# ABIDE IN ME

A Daughter's Illness, a Father's Struggle,
and a Reminder That the Miraculous
Isn't Just a Thing of the Past

## CHRIS SLAUGHTER

| Library of Congress Control Number: | | 2014918286 |
|---|---|---|
| ISBN: | Hardcover | 978-1-4990-8296-8 |
| | Softcover | 978-1-4990-8297-5 |
| | eBook | 978-1-4990-8298-2 |

**NIV**

Scripture quotations marked NIV are taken from the *Holy Bible, New International Version®. NIV®.* Copyright © 1973, 1978, 1984 by International Bible Society. Used by permission of Zondervan. All rights reserved. [Biblica]

This book was printed in the United States of America.

Rev. date: 10/17/2014

**To order additional copies of this book, contact:**
Xlibris LLC
1-888-795-4274
www.Xlibris.com
Orders@Xlibris.com
671528

# CONTENTS

But I knew—believed, at least—what I had learned about healing in those churches of Praise Jesus, The Lord Is Mighty, piney-woods amen corners much beloved by my twenty-two-year-old mother and my aunts: that healing is never about the healed or the healer, but about God's will. For one to rejoice at the sick made well is normal, quite the expected thing, but the person healed has an obligation to then ask why—to meditate on God's will, and the extraordinary lengths to which God has gone to realize His will. What did God want of me, in this case?

—Stephen King, *The Green Mile*

# Preface

I WANT TO START by confessing a major weakness: I'm quick to think I have it all figured out. That pride not only covers the routine situations of day-to-day life, but it transcends this place and time and encompasses my view of the God above us. I've been quick to argue with other Christians about His nature, His character, and the full measure of His divinity. I keep that weakness well hidden, of course, but only from the eyes of those around me, not from the vision of the One watching over us all.

If anything brings a proud father to the realization that he's more foolish than wise, it's the questions that arise when one of his children falls ill. I don't mean the kind of seasonal sicknesses that come and go each year or the occasional virus that keeps a kid in bed for a few days. Those ailments are exhausting and frustrating, but they are usually over in such short order that they aren't enough to interfere with my worldview.

On the other hand, when your daughter is diagnosed with an autoimmune disease and you have to put her on chemo at the age of six, the solidity of your conviction begins to wane. If you've always called God the protector of the weak, you struggle to speak with the determination you once had.

Then a year and a half later, literally on the eve of ending her chemo treatments, the same child is afflicted with a disease that no one can diagnose. As you set aside the celebration you thought you'd have after her first disease to watch her being wheeled in for an MRI or hold her down for a spinal tap, how do you still call Him the healer you always thought He was?

When shaken to the core after countless fears have assailed you over three years of your daughter's different afflictions, do you emerge from the depths of uncertainty unscathed, or do you possibly not emerge at all? Will you be able to silence the doubt in your mind and follow with your heart when, in the middle of your struggles, God calls to you and says "Abide in Me?"

# Chapter One

# Dominate

*DOMINATE*—THAT WORD HAS been part of a running joke in the Slaughter house after the birth of each of my children. Unlike the common comingling of two people found when new lives are created, my genetic code had entirely taken over. My son and daughter had my dark hair, green-blue-gold eyes, the absence of a chin, and nerdy obsession with learning new things. Out of kindness, people would try to find minor similarities the kids might have with my wife, Beth, but it was painfully obvious that they were all me. Beth always assured everyone that she was part of the birthing process, but if people hadn't actually seen that she was pregnant, no one would have believed her.

For the first few years of my little girl's life, she had my fair complexion and smattering of freckles. At an early age, she was already acquainted with our dermatologist because of the myriad of skin issues that came with my genetics. In time, though, everyone expected her to grow out of those problems and simply have to endure being pasty white and overly freckled for the remainder of her existence.

Then, in the summer of 2011, an attribute that's clearly all Beth emerged: beautifully tanned skin. My wife is one of those people most of us envy because she can go outside for half an hour and have noticeable tan lines. By the end of each summer, I'd always called Beth my little Mahican because of her perfect, glowing skin, and now Samantha could go by the same moniker. As the weeks passed, Sam's skin took on a homogenous bronzed tone, which was adorable on her athletic six-year-old frame and gave Beth a chance to brag about having a long-overdue contribution to our daughter's constitution. There was just one oddity: the outside of her right shin was slightly lighter than the rest of her leg. As I mentioned before, she'd always had skin issues, so we assumed it was another spot she'd irritated that would eventually heal and tan like the rest of her body. As the summer progressed, however, things took a turn in an unexpected direction. Not only was that spot not tanning, it was expanding across a larger part of her shin, and her skin was becoming opaque, growing nearly cadaverous in appearance. Coupled with the change in color, the texture of her skin roughened and was increasingly leathery. When late July rolled around, we decided to visit Sam's dermatologist to get a better understanding of what was happening to her leg.

It's worth taking a moment to mention that Samantha was quick to express her discontent with visiting doctors very early in life. We largely avoided our general practitioner for most run-of-the-mill illnesses, so when we did go, a well-child visit with a slew of shots was nearly always in store. When Sam was two and a half, it took my wife plus three nurses to hold her down for immunizations, and the emotional trauma of Sam crying out for her mother to help her was more than Beth cared to handle. By the age of three, Sam had developed enough core strength to necessitate me going along to pin her down for exams and injections. I was able to tuck away my emotions long enough to be impassive during the process and, knowing she was outgunned on the strength side, she was less likely to fight me as the syringes slipped into her skin.

Since the visit to the dermatologist, Dr. Amy Wood, was just to check on Sam's skin discoloration, I didn't accompany Beth because a wrestling match wasn't expected to be part of the equation. Based on some initial research we'd done, we thought she had either a pigmentation issue or something more serious (albeit purely aesthetic) called vitiligo, where skin loses its color over time. It wasn't until the doctor's visit that Beth sensed the problem was far more severe.

Instead of a routine visit and a prescription for steroids or other topical cream, the dermatologist wanted to do a biopsy of the affected area for further testing. She mentioned a few potential diagnoses but didn't want to worry us until she had confirmation from the lab, which is how doctors say there's a major issue. When discussing the biopsy, Dr. Wood attempted to communicate in a robust vocabulary to keep Samantha in the dark about the need to take a punch out of her shin. Sam has always been very intuitive, so she deciphered the cryptic conversation going on beside her, looked the doctor in the eyes, and said, "You're not taking a piece of my skin." While still in shock at Sam's understanding of what was to come, the doctor stepped out of the room to retrieve the utensils she'd need, which gave Beth time to talk to Samantha about remaining calm and still while the doctor did the biopsy.

While my daughter is fully capable of controlling her anger, she has a very strong sense of right and wrong and doesn't hesitate to lash out when injustice occurs. Beth quickly realized things were going to get ugly since Sam viewed carving into her leg as falling decidedly into the realm of wrong—absurd, I know. Dr. Wood walked in alone, required tools in hand, hoping that Sam would acquiesce to the flesh harvesting; but as soon as she approached the exam table, Samantha went ballistic. Amy quickly said some secret emergency word in a loud voice, and four nurses came pouring into the room in SWAT-team fashion. Holding my daughter down required all of them plus Beth, but Sam was controlled enough not to thrash with the leg where the sharp metal object was working its way into her skin.

With the needed flesh removed, the doctor set to the task of suturing Sam's leg; but she soon made a defeated face and set her tools down, opting to simply bandage the biopsy site instead. Amy later explained that Sam's skin was so taut and inelastic that when she attempted to stitch it, the skin shredded. That was neither what she'd expected nor a positive indicator for Sam's diagnosis.

It would be several days before the test results came back, but the tone of the appointment was clear: Dr. Wood knew something was seriously wrong. It was early the next week when my wife got a call that began with the words, "Well, we've confirmed that it's not cancerous, but . . ."

# Chapter Two

# Diagnosis

**PROGRESS NOTES** — **Formedic**

NAME: Samantha Slaughter

DATE - TIME / HT / CPT CODE / WT / BMI / BP / P / T / ALLERGIES: NKDA

8/15/11  1) "6" white, leathery area on leg
Hx of 4 months
⊕ Hx of eczema
⊕ Petroleum Jelly + OTC Anti-fungal

⊕ last visit last year or 2

MVI
fish oil

R/O morphea vs PIH vs eczema

Hx/o eczema
rapid increase in depigmentation leathery texture to ® calf

3mm punch close c̄ 5.0 if equivocal will send to Metry NP

Last seen 12/13/10

⊕ scaling of scalp ↑ frequency of shampoo to 2x a week samples taclonex scalp soln

(call)  Amy Wood NP

3mm punch
BX
R/O morphea vs PIH vs eczema

Date: Monday, 22 August 2011

Hey girls, we got Samantha's test results back, and the first thing they said was she doesn't have cancer! What? Who said we were testing for that! She has to go to a pediatrician that specializes in dermatology. She has morphea, which is thickening of the skin and loss of pigmentation, something that old people get. So they want to test internally to make sure she doesn't have this anywhere else in her body. I'm hoping they don't need to do any more testing on her because last Monday was pretty traumatic. Would you please pray with me that she will have complete healing before we even go to the dermatologist?

Love,
Beth

DURING THAT PHONE call, the nurse told Beth that Samantha was being diagnosed with a disease called linear morphea. She also found out that Dr. Wood called the chief of staff in the dermatology unit at Texas Children's Hospital to schedule an appointment for Sam as quickly as possible.

I remember thinking, *What the fill-in-the-blank is linear morphea?* I wanted to be sure I knew what it was when I got home so I could allay the mountain of fears sure to be crushing my wife after that call. She's the type that worries when laundry sits in the dryer for more than fifteen seconds after it's done, so I knew she'd be pacing the floor. Like any normal person in modern times, I went to the source of all things medical—the Internet.

I found that *morphea* is a broad term describing a myriad of afflictions, but I soon realized that the problem might be more than skin-deep. The disease itself is autoimmune in nature, thus the mention of cancer as a potential diagnosis. With morphea, instead of the body developing tumors, it overproduces collagen and forces it into places it doesn't belong. Her diagnosis was one that carried very heavy weight, with outcomes implying lifelong scarring of her leg, physical disability, or even death if the disease spread to her organs. The incidence of linear morphea was incredibly rare, afflicting as few as two or three children per million. Being a bit of a math nerd, I was already crunching numbers in my mind. I did the calculations around the improbability of her getting the disease (which was a few-in-a-million kind of thing) coupled with the potential that she had developed a worst-case version of it (another low-probability event), and I decided that having both of those things happen in tandem was a statistical impossibility. With that math in mind, I was feeling pretty good, all things considered.

After perusing a few more sites outlining descriptions, explanations, and expectations, I made the mistake of clicking the images tab. What I saw was heartbreaking. One picture after another showed malformed extremities, faces and chests, with irregular skin tones and disfigured body parts.

Then I stumbled upon the most startling photo of all—a carbon copy of my daughter's right leg. A giant white strip ran along the shin and thigh, just like Sam's. But the muscles were shrunken, half the size of the other leg. The leg was also shorter and bent outward where an opaque strip crossed the outside of the knee. I couldn't help but wonder how someone with a leg like that could walk at all, much less normally.

By the time I got home that evening, I was pleasantly surprised that Beth was less spun up than I expected. I wasn't about to derail her calm, so I told her that I would arrange the appointment at Texas Children's and double-check the credentials of the doctor we were going to see to ensure that it was the best place for Samantha to get treatment.

That night, with a budding fear for Sam's future in my heart, I slipped out of the house to work out and burn off some steam. An hour and a half of lifting weights helped put me more at ease, and I was in decent spirits when I walked back into the house. I looked for Beth downstairs but couldn't find her anywhere. As I walked past the bottom of the staircase, I heard a delicate noise coming from above. Halfway into my ascent to the second floor, I recognized the sound as Beth's gentle sobbing, a cacophony I am fortunate enough to hear very rarely. I pushed open the study door and found her staring at the same type of images I'd seen hours before. I turned off the monitor and pulled her into my arms as my sense of calm evaporated. Holding her from behind, her tears warmed the skin of my upper arm as she repeated between sobs, "That's her leg . . . that's her leg . . . that's her leg . . ."

It wasn't until early in the morning that I turned the screen back on and saw the website she was perusing. It was set up by lawyers getting people to file malpractice suits against physicians who failed to diagnose the illness in advance of permanent disabilities or even death. After looking at the propaganda on the website, Beth was convinced that Sam's morphea was so severe that it was going to kill her. What was it Shakespeare said in *Henry VI* about lawyers?

While I wanted to blame the makers of that website for using excessively graphic images, I quickly realized that the fault wasn't theirs; it was mine. On the night that we found out our daughter's serious diagnosis, I decided that working out was more important than discussing Sam's medical condition with my wife? Had I talked her through the diagnosis and given her some sense of comfort, she might not have gone online to search for answers on her own.

More frustrated than before, and despite the diagnosis and images, I wouldn't accept that Sam had that disease. This was the kid who hardly knew how to walk; she ran everywhere at full throttle. She did gymnastics three days a week and was looking forward to doing even more because she showed so much promise as an athlete. I'd made up my mind; they had to be wrong, and I was going to prove it.

# Chapter Three

# Tinkering

Date: Tuesday, 30 August 2011

So we had our appointment with the dermatologist today, and she prescribed a couple of medicines for us to use on Sam, which is great. The downside is that she still wants us to consult with another specialist at the hospital, just to be sure it's not internal. Since she's just a doctor for skin, we have to go to a rheumatologist who will take blood and rule out anything systemic. But the plus is that Samantha didn't have any skin removed or other tests today; she was so relieved (and so was I)!!! They said they could just use her old sample. She does have morphea and always will (even though it may be dormant for long periods), but she didn't seem as concerned as Dr. Wood was about it being something serious. She looked and felt all over her leg and asked about whether or not Sam was uncomfortable or limited in her range of motion, which was answered right away since she walked in on Sam doing backflips using Chris's hands. But she still wants to do more tests because it seemed to have spread so quickly.

I'm feeling much better, and Samantha had an awesome date with Mommy and Daddy today! Thanks for listening to me being a drama queen last night.

Love ya lots!
Beth

WHEN I WAS fourteen, a friend and I had plans to go to an indoor rock-climbing gym one afternoon. Being a couple years older than me, he was going to drive; but when I stepped out of his house, I found him standing in front of his mom's car with the hood up and his hands on his hips. Over the years, we'd rigged up all kinds of self-created remote-controlled cars and go-carts, but I'd never seen him fix a real car before. After a moment, he leaned forward, slid his hand over a couple of parts, did some tweaking, and stood back up to observe his handiwork. He stepped around to the driver's seat, slid in, turned the key, and absolutely nothing happened. He reemerged at the hood to repeat the process: reach in, tinker, try the ignition—all with no success. I finally walked over and asked, "What you are doing?" He looked up, smiled, and replied, "I have absolutely no clue." He turned his attention back to the car and began to tinker again.

As men, we tend to overestimate our problem-solving abilities, but we're proud enough not to let that interfere with our attempts to solve them anyway. In this regard, I'm far worse than most. I may not be the smartest guy in the room, but when it comes to fixing what's broken, I'm beyond tenacious. I only sleep three or four hours a night, so I have ample time to devote to projects, house repairs, studying obscure medical conditions, or feebly attempting to write a book. When Sam was diagnosed with linear morphea, it was an affliction I'd never heard of before. I'd taken the first step of familiarizing myself with the disease; the next step was to fix it.

As I've already mentioned, while some websites aren't exactly created by credible physicians, there are some reputable medical sites that offer a wealth of information on most diseases. You can learn what a diagnosis means, how it's confirmed, how it's treated, and a long-term prognosis—all in a matter of minutes. However, for more obscure illnesses such as Samantha's, things get a little dicey. First, the statistics about the disease start to diverge. Some sites suggested there was a two-in-a-hundred-thousand chance of having her affliction; others said it was closer to one in a million. The range of treatments widened as well, including creams, pills, steroids, chemotherapy, and potentially surgery to remove damaged parts of the body. The images of those afflicted followed suit, growing more disparate as I clicked through the Web's endless results. For some, I could see a subtle shift in pigmentation where a low-grade version of the disease struck, while some had one leg that was half the diameter and several inches shorter than the other. To combat my growing concern, instead of focusing on learning more about her diagnosis, I found myself looking for ways to disprove it.

After I exhausted the resources on the Web and felt less than confident in the information at the fringe of the Internet, I turned to more technical sources. I tracked down a publication on morphea as a whole, not just linear morphea, which listed abstracts from every major study or article on the disease over the last couple of decades. With a pencil and notepad on one side and a medical dictionary and *Gray's Anatomy* (which has nothing to do with the TV show) on the other, I started tinkering.

To say it was slow going would be a vast understatement. While both of my parents have PhDs in fields of science, and I periodically paid attention in high school biology classes, my understanding of technical medical terms was wildly lacking. I found myself grinding to a halt every few words to search for definitions or illustrations that would explain what I was reading. Ultimately, my natural obsessiveness and tenacity came into play during this period. I slept less, read more, and had half-legible notes scattered everywhere. Page after page, I crossed through illnesses that didn't fit or articles that led to a dead end and kept centering in on one thing. Linear morphea was the best fit. There were other possibilities, but nothing came together quite as well as her original diagnosis. I felt like C. S. Lewis, who was devout in his adolescent conviction as an atheist, but in 1929, "gave in and admitted that God was God." Like Lewis, I ended up believing the exact opposite of what I had hoped to be true.

Following two weeks of intense research, we saw a pediatric dermatologist at Texas Children's, which turned out to be a nonevent. We expected another extensive and invasive examination, but the physician simply looked at, measured, and touched Sam's leg. She then rather abruptly ended the appointment, telling us that we needed to schedule a follow-up visit with one of her colleagues, a pediatric rheumatologist. Beth and Sam were both elated that this appointment was quick and didn't involve any needles or scalpels, but the vibe I got from the doctor was not reassuring. I didn't see confidence in her eyes; I saw concern. It wasn't as if she was uncertain about what was happening; it was as if she didn't want to be the one to deliver the bad news. Another specialist, another appointment, and another two weeks of time to kill before our battle with her illness began. In other words, more time to kick the problem solving into overdrive.

That car we were tinkering with ended up starting, by the way. We had no idea what we touched or what made it suddenly do what we wanted it to do, but the rock climbing that afternoon was awesome. Sometimes things fix themselves in ways we can't understand, I suppose.

# Chapter Four

# MISSING

I N ONE OF my favorite movies, *The Usual Suspects*, Kevin Spacey's character says that "the greatest trick the devil ever pulled was convincing the world that he didn't exist." In the simplest terms, sin represents Satan's power to lead people away from God and into something lesser. I, most often, am led into myself. The slope of that descent is so subtle it usually begins with a step initiated by God to guide me down His path. Yet nearly without fail, I slip out of the copilot's chair and take a firm grip on the main controls myself. It isn't long before disaster ensues, which is when I usually follow Adam's lead after the fall in Genesis 3 and blame God for the failing since it was His plan all along, right?

As I recently drove to work, my mind was bouncing from one thing to another at a rapid-fire pace—schedules, plans, tasks to accomplish, and medical studies all swirling about at a dizzying speed. Yet no matter how many balls were in the air, I felt that I could juggle all of them with little trouble. Then I looked up, and a glitch in technology served as a means of divine communication.

In Houston, the major freeways are adorned with large black signs that allow the city to display messages covering a few lines of text. Generally, the notification crawling across the screen is traffic-related. It communicates scheduled roadwork, freeway closures, the time to the next major freeway, and even alerts you to accidents ahead so you can take another route to avoid traffic jams. It's a very handy feature, but its usefulness goes beyond convenience at times.

The two major exceptions to the traffic notifications are Amber Alerts and Silver Alerts. The first lets you know that a child has gone missing; the second is when someone suffering from Alzheimer's or Dementia goes missing. In the South, the tendency to take care of our own and look out for one another is deeply rooted; so when the board lights up, people take notice. That morning, a Silver Alert was issued for someone in Lufkin, Texas—a city about a hundred miles north of Houston. The screen flashed a license plate number, car description, and a way to reach the Lufkin police to report sightings. Just as I started to look away, the board began to cycle through with another message, but instead of populating the full screen, only three capital letters lit up: S-I-N. A moment later, the other bulbs kicked in, and that SIN turned out to be part of the word MISSING. I had never before noticed how those three letters reside in the midst of the larger word, but it shook me from my self-focused thought process and into a moment of revelation.

I found that billboard to be highly indicative of the nature of sin. If it were wildly obvious, we wouldn't do it—at least not as often or extensively. But because it is tucked away in the midst of something seemingly innocuous, we don't notice it until it's shoved in our faces and exposed for what it is. My sins fall heavily into this camp, particularly with my tendency to take control of situations and guide or manipulate them to the places I believe they should go. In Samantha's case, I was going to fix her illness. I'd do the research, I'd work with the doctor, and I'd do whatever it took to completely heal her. Though my efforts started out focused on my daughter, it didn't take long before it was all about me and my abilities.

When we're deeply immersed in problem solving, we have a tendency to crowd out God. I had such a strong handle on everything around me that I'd not left Him much room to work. My sin started as a divinely ordained drive to protect Sam, but my desire to wrestle control away from God tainted the purity of that role and morphed into an obsession with manifesting a specific outcome, with or without His help.

When I'm immersed in fixing things, it is incredibly difficult to take a step back and recognize when the path I'm traversing tilts away from God. This subtle shift is one of the ways that the devil does his best work. I not only fail to realize I'm sinning, I believe that I'm following God more closely than I ever have before.

Part of me wishes I had an internal billboard, like the one on the highway, to flash those three letters whenever I started to head down the wrong path. That said, another part of me wouldn't be a big fan of that at all because it would muddle my plans, interfere with my successes, and force me to ease my grip on the reins during periods of crisis. Deep down, I know that God's will is going to be done. His work isn't dependent on me, so why not be a conduit for His plan by submitting to His will and taking part in something greater than myself? The answer to that question is simple: fear. Fear of failure, fear of the wrong outcome, fear of loss of my loved ones. It is the fear that keeps my knuckles whitened with my grip on each day and blinds me to the sin hiding in the midst of the purported good surrounding it.

Fear is a very powerful weapon, yet its greatest potency isn't found in the paralysis it can induce but, rather, in its ability to move us out of the present. In C. S. Lewis's book *The Screwtape Letters*, he focuses in on this aspect of distraction with wonderful clarity. Instead of allowing us to react, respond, and adapt through communion with God during difficult times, fear projects our thoughts from the concrete realm of what is and into the yet-to-be nightmare of what may be. This is a struggle for nearly all of us—one that makes us easy to exploit, distract, and guide down paths we were never intended to tread.

I was so busy focusing on healing my daughter that I'd made more than a few oversights in my role as a husband, something I vowed to repeat as infrequently as possible. While I could honestly have used the moral support, I needed to think about my role as my wife's protector and whether or not to have Beth join me at the upcoming visit with the rheumatologist at Texas Children's. After all of my research, I knew that the appointment would be long, tedious, and involve discussions about extreme outcomes that I'd rather not introduce into Beth's already concerned mind until it was absolutely necessary.

# Chapter Five

# Dr. Eyal Muscal

THIS IS THE list of topics and questions I took to Sam's first appointment with the rheumatologist—the product of many sleepless nights and excessive medical journal reading. The strikethroughs, question marks, and legible writing belong to Dr. Muscal.

Muscal – 9/13/11 @ 10:00
6621 Fannin (at Bates)
Entrance 10
11th Floor
832-824-3830

Ruled out:
~~Melasma~~ (darkening pigment)
~~Borrelia~~ (no bulls-eye, not pink)
~~Lichen sclerosus~~ (vulvar, rarely pediatric)
~~Polymiositis~~ (no obvious muscle loss)
~~Fibrosing basal-cell carcinoma~~ (benign biopsy result)
~~Atrophic abortive morphea~~ (Not dark, texture difference)
~~Bulbus morphea~~ (no ulcers)
~~IAPP~~ (loss of pigment, but normally on the back, texture not the same)
Nodal scleroderma (no keloids)
~~Mycosis fungoides~~ (appearance, benign, mostly males, over 20)

Possible:
Vitiligo
Eosinophilic fasciitis or Shulman's (stress, thickening, warm) _____ (?)
    Complimentary or stand-alone?
    Only fascia involved or also dermal?
Panscleratic morphea (no tank top)

Most likely:
Linear morphea
    Lack of pigmentation
    Size of area
    Textural difference
    4x as often in females
    Higher incidence in whites
    Raynaud's syndrome                          *not systemic*
        Exclusively in systemic or also in localized (W)
        If positive, not Shulman's

Testing:
√ Antinuclear antibody (ANA) test                *kidney*
    Anticentromere                               *liver*
        60% of limited systemic, 15% of diffuse  *Blood*
        Predictive of limited cutaneous involvement
        Range of 0.0 to 0.9
            Level suggestive of anything specific?
    Anti-scl 70 (ATA)
        More severe systemic issue

Thursday + Friday

Do patients have one or the other or both?
    Meaning of having both?
    Antihistone antibodies (AHAY) *NO*
       Traditionally for lupus
    HLA presence (PSS)
    CD34 (absence or reduction) *NO*
— Ultrasound to determine muscle involvement?
Method of analyzing bone involvement?
CREST attributes?
    Raynaud's
Other testing now or in the future? *NO*

Infusion center
vs
Home visit

CT or MRI

Treatment:
    UVA -1 ~ ? wright
       Degrades collagen matrix
       Immunosuppressive?
    Psaloren
    Acitretin (psoriasis)
    Calcipotrial
    ~~Penicillin G (IM)~~
    ~~Depenicillamine~~
    ~~Cyclosporine~~
    Photochemotherapy
    ~~Sulfasalazine (SSZ)~~
General immunosuppressive treatment
    Public school
    Duration of treatment 1-2 yrs
    Oral, injection, topical
    Methotrexate ↓ liver

IV

2 wk ———————— injection or
4 wk                     subcutaneous
                              shot

Other:
    Duration of illness
    Signs it is abating
    Recurrence after initial infection

Steroids (weekly IV)
   ↳ Shots

Photos
Dr. Reni's #
Insurance

Metho:
ulcers (oral)
Infection
Nauseaus
—————
Shots

Steroid:
Catabolic
Hairy
weight gain
4-6 wks IV
↳ Shot

In the final days leading up to Sam's appointment with the rheumatologist, I knew what I had to do. After all the digging and tinkering, I'd come to the conclusion that Sam not only had linear morphea, but a very serious case of it. If I was right, it would mean that the least aggressive of treatment plans would involve chemotherapy but that things might be bad enough to require surgery, which may still fail to stop the progression of her disease. On top of that, when considering some of Sam's other odd symptoms, there was a chance she had something systemic, not just something affecting her leg. If it was systemic, it could ultimately impact the function of her organs, and there was a chance it could kill her. Needless to say, the physician and I were going to have a somber conversation about a lot of scary things. Samantha had to go; there was no question about her attendance. It was Beth that I increasingly viewed as an optional participant. The more I thought and prayed about it, the more I realized I didn't want her to be afraid for Sam or hear words like surgery or mortality rate. Now for the hard part: convincing Beth not to attend the most important doctor's visit in her daughter's life.

I was shocked by how painless and calm the conversation with Beth turned out to be. I laid out my thoughts on Samantha's condition, omitting some of the more alarming parts that were yet unconfirmed. I told her it was going to be a highly technical appointment that would bore her to tears and that if she spent the afternoon with Noah, he could get some much-needed attention since our recent focus had been almost entirely on Sam. I also didn't know how long the visit would take; it could easily span several hours, leaving Noah in the lurch for transportation at the end of school. Being the list maker that she is, we sat down, and she walked me through all of the questions she wanted answered, most of which I already had on my own list. She knew that I was taking this very seriously, and it was almost as if my hyperfocused attitude allowed her to take a step back and be less concerned about how that particular visit would go.

As the day approached, I continued to write down questions about alternate diagnoses, tests to confirm or rule out various conditions, and tried not to focus too heavily on the depth of treatments Sam might be forced to endure.

On the day of the appointment, we went to the rheumatology department on the eleventh floor at Texas Children's. As soon as you step foot in that hospital, you realize that things can always be worse than they are. In every direction, you see children with afflictions ranging from mild to completely debilitating. Samantha's eyes were perpetually scanning, ever processing the conditions of the children around her in an obvious attempt to not only see what was wrong with them but to ultimately decipher just how bad things might be for her.

When our name was called, we ventured beyond a blue-tinged wall and into the wing devoted to bone and joint ailments. After taking Sam's vitals, we were ushered into an exam room, where we waited for the doctor to join us. As with all appointments up to that point, I'd done my homework on the physician we were seeing. Aside from the usual check on his background, areas of expertise, and education, I went so far as to have my mother (a dean at the Baylor College of Medicine) check with the chief of staff at Texas Children's and find out everything she could about Dr. Eyal Muscal. Both from what I'd found and what she'd heard, Samantha would be in very good hands. Within the first few minutes of what turned into an hour-long exam, I realized that I couldn't have asked for a better doctor for my daughter.

From the onset, he not only displayed a good bedside manner with Samantha, but he also was very keenly focused on wanting to hear what both she and I had to say about her illness. I'd taken the time to meet with Dr. Wood in Kingwood and brought the medical records from that practice with me. When I passed them over to him, he arranged the papers neatly and then unexpectedly set them on a nearby chair without looking through them. His philosophy was simple: he trusted parents and kids more than he trusted doctors. Though he gave the notes from her previous visit with the Texas Children's dermatologist a cursory glance, he didn't want to be biased by what was in a file. He wanted to see where the conversation and examination went and then consider the full depth of what the records had to say to corroborate what he learned during our discussion.

Along with the medical file, I'd brought the product of my own research with me, complete with random scribbling and a battery of other questions and concerns I'd amassed in the weeks leading up to the appointment. This paper, he did not simply set aside. He took it from my hands, pulled out his pen, huddled next to me, and went through every single line of the two-page-long document. As we perused the list, he would stop to explain why something didn't quite fit, note areas

DR. EYAL MUSCAL

where he was uncertain, and circle parts that he thought were worth looking into more thoroughly. But as he drew near the end of the document, he saw my conclusion that she likely had a serious form of linear morphea and shook his head in agreement as he absentmindedly stared at Sam's cadaverous right leg. Coming back into the moment, he then began his own line of questioning. The queries spanned her eating habits, physical abilities, hobbies, levels of discomfort, and everything else you can imagine. That portion of the conversation lasted over fifteen minutes, with the questions coming rapid-fire once he and I settled into a surprisingly natural rhythm of Q&A.

Once his questions were answered, he began the task of physically examining my daughter. The first thing I noticed and immediately respected was the depth of his thoroughness. Sam sat on the exam table, allowing him to take measurements of both of her legs. The surface area of her leg the disease covered was massive, beginning on the top of her right foot, up the center of her ankle, spanning the outer aspect of her shin, trailing along the outside of her knee, and then up a part of her thigh. Given the size of the area, he was forced to make pen marks on Sam's legs (a game she liked) to remember where he'd begun a measurement because tracking it with his eyes and fingers grew challenging. With the equivalent of a tailor's measuring tape, he painstakingly evaluated the length and circumference of her legs at various points over and over again. After that, he tested the elasticity of her skin, attempting to pinch up small areas (a game she didn't like) to see if the flesh had any give. In most places, he was unable to grasp even a fraction of an inch of excess skin due to the ever-growing mass of collagen beneath the surface of her flesh. Coupled with the large area affected and the crossing of joint lines, the lack of excess skin was a bad sign in terms of diagnosing the severity of her disease. With the measurement and visual exam complete, he asked Sam to get off of the table and walk around the room for the first time.

The look on his face wasn't quite one of shock, but it conveyed a deep interest and some degree of surprise. After she did a series of movements and exercises in the room, we went into the hallway where she could cover a more meaningful distance, allowing him to observe her gait, balance, and speed. She walked heel to toe, on her tippy-toes, on her heels, squatted and walked like a duck, hopped like a kangaroo, and a slew of other movements designed to demonstrate whether or not her joints and muscles were being impacted. After nearly ten minutes, Sam made a disenchanted face when he told her we were done with that part of the testing, and we headed back into the room.

As we took our seats, he was obviously deep in thought, so I waited silently while he arranged the words floating through his mind. When he spoke, it was with a measure of confused awe in his voice. He confirmed that she was almost certainly afflicted by linear morphea, but he also stated that it was unlikely hers had the potential to be systemic, ruling out concerns of a mortality rate. He went on to say that if he had seen pictures of her leg and known the measurements of the area it covered, his expectations would have been wildly different than what he found in Samantha. He would have anticipated constant discomfort, alterations in gait, loss of balance, and differences in the circumference of her legs due to inhibited muscle growth on the affected side. She had none of those. Both legs were identical in length and circumference; she moved with alacrity and grace and was still routinely doing gymnastics without a single complaint of pain. That, in and of itself, he found utterly amazing.

However, he cautioned, the likelihood that nothing was going on beneath the surface of such an aggressively growing area of skin was very, very small. Given how quickly the disease was moving, he wanted to begin treatments within the next couple of weeks, even before we understood what was happening to her muscles and bones. Though I knew what that meant, my heart still dropped when the words *chemotherapy* and *steroids* were spoken aloud. The regimen he felt would be most effective involved weekly infusions of both of those drugs, coupled with a daily antimalarial pill to help with inflammation and two tablets of folic acid to help with nausea and ward off some of the damage the chemo could cause her liver. After that, he migrated into the realm of maybes. She may or may not handle the chemo well, may or may not lose her hair, may or may not have trouble vomiting, and may or may not fall ill on a very frequent basis once the infusions began. He expected the cycle of infusions to last at least three months; after which we could evaluate their efficacy and possibly migrate to a lower dosage of chemo through at-home injections. To convey the words that followed, his voice softened, and he expressed his concern that the drugs may not stop the disease's progression, and we may have to consider more "aggressive" alternatives. With hushed voices, we discussed the possibility of surgery to remove tainted muscles and sections of bone in the hopes that it would alter the trajectory of her affliction. Even then, there was a strong possibility that our efforts would fail to reverse damage already done and that she would ultimately be physically disabled. One likely form of disability would be a joint contracture, leaving her with a leg that would shift outward at her knee and/or ankle. Another expectation was limited bone growth on her right side during the one- to three-year life cycle of the disease, ultimately leaving her with one leg shorter than the other. It took less than a second for the pictures of deformed children from the Internet to flourish, but I pushed the images from my mind and refocused on the conversation at hand.

At this point, Dr. Muscal stepped out of the doctor role and shifted to a more fatherly tone (having little girls himself), advising me to think about everything we'd discussed, to confer with my wife and give him a call back when we felt we might be ready to start the infusions of chemo and steroids. I stood silently for a moment before meeting his eyes and asking, "What time should we be here tomorrow?" He was taken aback, then expressed his understanding that I wanted to move quickly but said that waiting a few extra days to speak with Beth likely wouldn't make a difference in the long run. He told me that with a diagnosis of this severity, there's usually a "grieving period" that he would expect us to require. Again, my response was simple. I didn't need a conference with Beth to decide what was best for Samantha's healing; my wife would trust my judgment, and I wanted to start treatments as soon as we possibly could. He smiled, shook his head, and led me to the nurse's station to schedule the first round of infusions. The next day was booked solid, but the day after had a 12:00 p.m. appointment, which I took without delay. Dr. Muscal and I shook hands and stepped away from one another, realizing it would be the first of many encounters we would share on the long road ahead.

After discussing the appointment that day with Beth, she was reassured by Eyal's surprise at Sam's unchanged mobility, the absence of pain, and the speed with which we'd start treatments for her affliction. She was obviously still terrified for Sam's well-being; but having confirmation of the disease, some assurance it wasn't systemic, and a clear path forward helped calm the tempestuous sea of uncertainty we'd been in for nearly two months.

Very late that night, I crept into Samantha's room as she slept, something that would become commonplace for me in the months to follow. I knelt at the side of her bed, placed my hand on her shin, and prayed that her leg alone was affected. My mind was already picturing her with a disfigured limb, planning out the transition from gymnastics to piano lessons, and even thinking that we'd have to stop taking vacations to the beach and start going to the mountains, where an elevator shoe could be more easily concealed by clothing. It was with those thoughts in mind that I heard her ask, "What are you doing, Daddy?" With tears in my eyes obscured by the darkness of her room, I responded, "Just praying for your leg, kiddo." She laughed a little and, without a doubt in her mind, whispered, "You don't need to do that, I already know my leg is going to be perfectly fine," before rolling over and drifting off to sleep again.

The first two words that came to mind were sharp, *foolish girl*. If only she'd read what I'd read and knew what I knew, if only she was aware of how bad it was going to get, she wouldn't be so dismissive. Part of me wanted to tell her about the gravity of the situation so she would appreciate the time she had before it hit her full force. But as a father protecting his little girl, I couldn't possibly burst her bubble, no matter how uninformed her opinion may have been. Along with that thought, I recalled a quote from the Bible that I'd always found out of character for the normally love-laced words of the speaker. In remembering it, I opted to heed Jesus's warning when it comes to tainting the faith of children. If you've not read Matthew 18:6, it's worth a look, especially if you think the mob is the one who came up with "swimming with the fishes" concept.

Despite the upcoming infusion, I would try to keep her innocence and optimism intact as long as I possibly could. Instead of trying to heal her, I found myself focused on guarding the purity of her soul, no matter what happened to her leg.

# Chapter Six

# Pressure Cooker

Date: Tuesday, 13 September 2011

I'm totally freaking out. Let me fill you guys in . . .

Samantha was diagnosed with linear morphea, a rare autoimmune disease where the body starts to overproduce collagen for reasons no one fully understands. The form of disease Sam has is one that is only expected to be present on her right leg, where it is right now. If left untreated, it has the potential to alter the muscle and bone development of her shin, knee, ankle, and thigh on the right side of her body. To halt the progression of her morphea, she is going to start on an immunosuppressant and a steroid; both of which will be delivered through an IV at Texas Children's once a week. That will probably last six to twelve weeks, after which we'll continue to give her medicine at home, most likely through injections.

While it's definitely a scary time, knowing she doesn't have anything life threatening is such a blessing. Please pray for her strength as she goes through these treatments, our sanity as we try to figure out how to make this as unnoticeable as possible for Sam, and for her healing as we start her on those medicines. I may also need to dial back playtime together because she's going to have to be more careful about germs once she starts on the methotrexate.

I am incredibly grateful for all of the friendships I have with you guys. I can't tell you how comforting it is to know you're all praying for her. I love you guys.

Beth

WHEN I WAS young, it's not so much that my family was poor as it was frugal, though we were nowhere near living the high life. Both of my parents were from rural towns in Louisiana; neither of whom had overwhelming levels of wealth. My father's town was no more than a blinking light on the highway, my mother's just a bit larger but not exactly a booming metropolis. My folks were the first in their families to pursue PhDs, but even with stable jobs and income after college, they spent cautiously in my formative years. Nowhere was their frugality more evident than in our grocery shopping trips. We weren't just your average coupon clippers. Sure, we spent part of every Sunday carving up the newspaper and slipping little shards of paper into the light brown, accordion-style files in which coupons were kept. And yes, we took advantage of the nearby store's double- or triple-coupon nights, which were always a source of excitement. But the place where our cost cutting was most pronounced were the gypsy-like trips we would take on the weekends to get the best deal on specific items. Dietary staples like Diet Coke, Fruity Pebbles, Hamburger Helper, and potted meat were purchased so often that it was deemed financially rational to burn gas money (this was when gas was $0.99 a gallon) driving across town to hit a handful of stores in a single day. While some off-label products are just as good as the expensive ones, one place where frugality is painfully obvious is cuts of fresh meat. There were no T-bones or filet mignons; it was the low-priced, leatherlike meats for us. Fortunately, growing up in Louisiana, my mother was well versed in the art of pressure cooking.

As a kid, the pressure cooker was a very simple device. It was a deep silver pot, with a flimsy rubber ring along the inside of a small groove along the top and a long black handle that locked into place to create an airtight seal with the base. With the use of a little water and heat, one could render even the most unsavory cuts of meat palatable. Another feature of the pot was a tiny protrusion on top with a little hole cut into it, capped with a thimblelike piece of metal. I remember watching my mother cooking, the thimble dancing about on top of the pot when the steam inside built up and forced its way out. I also remember seeing when the pressure got so high that my mother would reach up, push the thimble to the right, and a stream of scalding steam would come blasting out, shooting down and to the left. I asked why she had to do that, and she said that sometimes, the pot built up so much pressure that if you didn't let some out, the whole thing just might explode.

During my younger years, I wasn't the best at anger management, a facet of my personality that my parents recognized early on. The notes from school about potentially being expelled for fighting helped clue them in, I suppose. In an attempt to counter my innate violence, they made me sit and read long books, ball up pieces of paper until they were the consistency of tissues, and even attempted having me take up sewing at one point. Why they thought giving me a sharp metal object during fits of rage was a good idea, I'll never understand! When that didn't do the trick, they tried other activities that required enough concentration that they hoped I'd forget whatever upset me. Nothing really worked, though, until they put a punching bag in the garage. After the luxury of getting a punching bag, there wasn't much left to spend on gloves, so we just had cheap hand wraps. On days when I wasn't in the best of moods, I could go outside, spend some time swinging, and before long, I found myself more at ease. That method of relieving stress became a habit, and I've had a punching bag ever since.

Though I can now slough off most frustrations with a combination of deep breathing, listening to music, reading, and running, there are certain situations that require burning off a bit more steam. The more articles I read with statistics pointing down the path of a permanent disability, the more the steam built up and the harder it was to get it out of my system using kinder, gentler methods. Sam's upcoming MRI was a crucial mile-marker on the road ahead, and my stress about what it would ultimately tell us was building rapidly. From a statistical perspective, everything about her condition suggested the MRI would reveal some degree of muscle and bone involvement. As Sam's illness seemed to progress aggressively, and the bad news continued to pour in, I found myself using the punching bag more and more frequently.

Initially, after I'd put the kids to sleep and slipped into the garage, I would just spend longer than normal working on the heavy bag. As I moved further down the path of silent rage, I found that even half an hour of punching with the thin leather gloves I usually wore wasn't enough; but if I removed the gloves, something about the sting of my flesh on the canvas was comforting. I knew that probably wasn't a healthy thing, but the catharsis was there, and I wasn't doing any serious damage to anyone, myself included. But as time passed and I grew increasingly concerned, even that was no longer enough.

I'm not sure why I got this idea, but one night, while the kids were sleeping, Beth was out with friends, and I had some time to myself, my eyes fell on the woodpile I keep in the corner of the garage. The massive stack of timber there is a by-product of trees I've cut down at various times on our one-acre lot. After using a chain saw to drop the trees, I cut them into logs, then split them into firewood to use in Houston's version of winter. Without really thinking, I slipped a drill from its resting place, traded the screwdriver tip for a drill bit, and bored a hole straight through the center of an oak log. After unhooking the punching bag from the chains holding it in place on the stand, I ran a rope through the log and tied a small noose on the top. I then threaded the rope through the upper part of the stand, and when I stepped back, the forty-pound canvas bag had been replaced by a several-foot-long log suspended four feet above the ground. I slipped the thin leather gloves on and began testing the resiliency of my makeshift target, only to find that it served its purpose perfectly. I felt every swing, from the ache in my knuckles to the dull reverberation through the bones of my hands. On occasion, I'd hit the log off-center, sending it spinning around in circles, leading to a painful collision when I landed a fist along the hardened core of the wood. Impressed with my creation and wanting to test the full extent of discomfort it could create, I slipped in a pair of earphones, blaring with the kind of music nice Christian boys don't listen to, and pulled off the gloves.

The first solid connection between my bare fist and the bark of the log sent a sharp pain along my knuckles, and I knew that I'd created a tiny fissure in the skin where the punch landed. While any normal person would have eased their intensity, I found myself punching harder and faster than before. I'd finally created a release that could distract me long enough to provide some semblance of peace from the thoughts that plagued me night and day. I kept swinging, and it was in this state that I found myself looking over my shoulder, into the face of my less-than-understanding wife.

I have a myriad of eccentricities that manifest themselves on a routine basis, so after all of our years together, shocking Beth with my behavior is something of a challenge; but what I was doing was past peculiar and drifting into the realm of disturbing. It was a combination of pain, confusion, and concern that drifted behind her eyes. Her words were few but dead-on, "I don't know if you're doing that because you want to hurt something or because you want something to hurt you, but neither one of those is a good thing."

Frankly, I didn't know either; I only knew that it felt like it was helping at the time. As she made her way into the house from the garage, my jaw tensed; I turned back around, and my already tattered knuckles slammed into the bark of the oak log again and again, thinking like Rockefeller that I just needed a little bit more to sate my appetite. She knew better, though. She knew that rage wouldn't beget peace; it would simply beget more rage. I thought I was tipping the thimble to the side and easing the pressure, but she understood that I was practically gluing the release valve down and pushing myself closer to an explosion.

# Chapter Seven

# First Infusion

Date: Wednesday, 21 September 2011
Subject: Sam's New iPod

I wanted to be sure your friends knew just how much I appreciate them taking care of Samantha while she's enduring treatments at the hospital. They've always been a source of laughter, fun, psychosis, and absolutely awesome pictures from mom prom—oh yes, I've seen them. But when they gather together to find ways to make sure Sam is distracted and enjoys her time at Texas Children's, it reminds me of just how amazing, compassionate, and selfless they all are.

In the span of a week, we've felt so many emotions: terrified of her diagnosis and all the things it's turned out not to be; brokenhearted over the treatments she has to endure; concerned about how she'd handle IVs, pills, shots, and side effects; and all the questions that swirl in our minds when we see someone we love suffering for reasons we can't even begin to understand. Yet through it all, we've felt the overwhelming peace of the intercessory prayers of others, seen courage in Sam that we didn't know she had, and watched as the body of Christ has joined together, moving as one to be sure we have everything we could possibly need or even want at a time like this.

The look on Sam's face when she opened that package and realized what they'd given her was absolutely priceless. Who would have thought our shy little nerd would love all this attention from everyone? Just before I put her to bed last night, she asked when she'd "get to" (not have to) go to the doctor again. When I told her it would be Thursday, she frowned a bit because she knew she had two days until then, and she wanted to play with her iPod sooner than that. Then she asked if she'd have to get a shot again, and I told her, "Yes, it would be just like last time." Her response was, "Oh well, it doesn't even hurt, and now I get to play Angry Birds the whole time." Knowing she's comfortable with everything that's going on is such a relief and takes away a burden we thought would last the entire six weeks that we're doing IVs, so I can't thank the girls enough for all the wonderful things they are doing to take care of our little girl.

Be sure to thank all of them for me even if they've just accelerated the "you're ruining my life phase" that's bound to come the first time I take that thing away for some reason. I thought I'd be able to avoid that until she turned thirteen . . .

Chris

IF YOU RECALL from a few chapters before, Samantha's August doctor's visit where a biopsy was required went less than smoothly. She screamed, she kicked, and it took nearly half a dozen people to control her to remove a small piece of her skin. With only two days to prepare for Sam's first infusion, Beth and I went to work on a game plan to manage the impending crisis we were certain to endure. I forced myself to tuck away my brewing rage and focus on the task at hand.

After speaking with the nurses in the infusion center, I learned that the IVs themselves would take at least two hours to run, perhaps more. In medical terms, that *always, always, always* means it's going to take longer. Beth and I wrestled with how we'd keep Samantha still and entertained for that long and, by and large, came up empty-handed every time. Ultimately, we decided that if (make that *when*) she decided to fight, I would sit behind her in the chair, bear-hug her to keep her as still as possible, and hold her there until her rage subsided and she tolerated the IV in her arm without being restrained.

When I made the commitment to do more as a protector for my wife and daughter, I decided that I would be there for every infusion or doctor's visit from then on. In corporate America, that can be something of a feat, but I was utterly amazed by the support I received from the team at NRG. Not only was there no judgment when I abdicated my role in a fairly sizeable acquisition, but I was advised to take as much time as needed to care for my family, trusting that whatever work I couldn't get to would be handled by those around me. I want to point out that this level of support didn't just come from close friends. I got calls from the treasurer, chief risk officer, and other high ranking employees—all asking me to explain what was happening and occasionally telling me that my family would be in their prayers.

For Sam's first infusion, I took the entire day off, allowing me to drop both kids off at school and spend a little time at home before collecting Samantha and driving her into town for her treatment. Surprisingly, though we knew the day was going to be both physically and emotionally taxing for all of us, Beth and I were in good spirits when we climbed into the car at the house to go get Sam from school. Then, unexpected and interesting things started to happen. The first came out of nowhere and had the potential to be a serious problem: Beth's car wouldn't start. I turned the key, pumped the gas, and did all of the things a guy with no mechanical knowledge would do—all to no avail. Then suddenly, after a few moments of waiting, the engine roared to life (as much as an Acadia can roar), and Beth and I subtly laughed at the minor interference. Next was a click of the garage door opener, which also didn't work. Beth kept trying the button while I got out to manually release and lift the garage door open. Just as my hand found the release lever, the button Beth was pressing started working again, and the door slid along its track to allow us an exit. After picking up Sam, we hopped onto the freeway to make our way into town, only to find a traffic jam in our path due to an accident between our house and the hospital. While the third issue wasn't a huge surprise, the other two had never happened until that morning.

Coincidentally, or not so coincidentally, Beth finished reading a book on spiritual warfare only a few days earlier. I'd read *The Invisible War* quite some time before, but it instantly popped into my mind as problem after problem arose, attempting to interfere with our mood on a very important day. In one passage, the author, Chip Ingram, referenced all the times that he'd been in the midst of profound spiritual growth, only to suffer one random form of interference after another. While I know the concept of spiritual warfare gives people the heebie-jeebies, it's one that I feel compelled to mention based on our experience. I also think that if you read the Bible, you can't possibly ignore the multitude of verses that make mention of darker forces present in this world that will assail us over the course of this life. Just to put things into context, the word *angel* appears 326 times in the Bible while the words *devil, demon*, and *Satan* show up 202 times; so if you tally the words, you've got two devils for every three angels. I mentioned I'm a math nerd, right? Don't get me wrong, I'm not trying to quantify the number of players on each team, I'm just making the point that you can't talk about the protection provided by angels without considering the things from which they're protecting us. During this time, the barrage of assaults on our sense of peace rose to a fever pitch, yet we experienced an inexplicable level of calmness. Because we were already expecting it and discussed it as a couple, we were prepared when it arose. I haven't really talked to a pastor about this yet, but at some point, I may ask about the theological implications of dropping an f-bomb on Satan. There were moments when my frustration level was high and my fear was running rampant, but when I recognized the source was anything but divine, I may or may not have said such a word to call out its origin and send it back from whence it came—which, I'll admit, was oddly relieving and effective at diffusing my negativity. Whether God would openly cheer on that kind of behavior or groan and slap his forehead at the gracelessness of my approach, I'm not quite sure. I'll add that to my ever-growing list of questions to be answered when I'm past this place and into the next.

Eventually, we pressed through the traffic, took the familiar route to the hospital, and made our way to the third floor where the infusion center is housed. We passed through the food court, beyond a pair of double doors, and with timidity, stepped into the horseshoe-shaped section of the hospital where kids with serious diseases go to get IVs. The arrangement was pretty straightforward: about a dozen small curtained-off areas with chairs/beds, each of which had their own TV and sitting area. Walking from the entrance to the nurse's station, we passed a few occupied beds and were instantly grateful for the relative health of our daughter despite her illness. I could feel Beth's mounting tension about how Sam would react to being hooked up to IVs, having her blood drawn, and handling the chemicals she was about to receive for the first time. We'd brought a myriad of distractions—DVDs, games, books, and a stuffed animal (which she affectionately named Muscal, after her rheumatologist); but we didn't know if it would be enough to keep Sam calm and comfortable.

As I looked around, the first thing that stood out was the amazing attitude of the staff. They were laid-back, constantly laughing, and wonderful with the kids scattered around the room. They moved with the grace and confidence that come from years of practice, which helped put everyone more at ease. The nurses could tell Samantha was apprehensive but didn't express any concern about how that would impact her infusions; they acted like she'd love every second of it. When the time came for them to slide a needle into her arm, the nurse told Samantha that it wasn't going to hurt much but that it might be best to look away. I knew Sam had no intention of being caught unaware, so I wasn't surprised at all when she let the nurse know she was going to watch everything.

At this point, I'd moved into a much closer position, both of my hands touching different parts of Sam's arm, ready to instantly pin it in place when her resistance began. Beth sat by my side, one of her hands pressed to my upper arm, mostly to assure herself of my ability to be strong if Sam started fighting and I had to spring into action. As the nurse slipped the needle into my daughter's vein, Samantha didn't scream, cry, or even flinch. She watched with calm curiosity as the needle went in and, with more focused interest, when the nurse told her she was going to draw some blood for the doctors to test. Since Sam didn't react with her typical violence in this kind of situation, I took the opportunity to start explaining what they were doing and why it would be helpful. As the nurse pressed the first test tube in, deep crimson liquid started to fill the vial, and when I told Sam that was her blood pouring out, her mouth curved into a tiny grin, and she said a single word, "Cool." Up until then, Beth had kept her composure, but on hearing that word, she ducked her head behind Sam's chair and quietly wept tears of relief. The entire visit wouldn't go quite so smoothly, but it had begun with far less agony than expected.

All the worrying we'd done, all my planning about the best way to pin her down when the fight began was utterly wasted time. I find that I do that perpetually. I'm always so busy imagining how to react to the failures to come that I waste time I could otherwise enjoy during pivotal moments. It's an ongoing lack of faith I demonstrate, once again saying that I not only know the outcome but can preplan what needs to be done instead of talking to God about it and embracing each moment without wasting time condemning the days of the future.

While Sam's initial reaction was unexpectedly good, the rest of the visit grew tumultuous. The steroids started to have an effect within fifteen minutes, causing her nausea, agitation, and restlessness. After that came a bag of saline to clean out her blood vessel before the chemo infusion began. The bag in which the medicine arrived was emblazoned with bold letters of CHEMOTHERAPY and a warning to anyone who might come in contact with it. Coupled with that, it was delivered in a bag within a larger, heartier bag, clearly indicating that if someone was exposed to it, the results would be less than pleasant. Seeing all of that and watching as they prepared to send it coursing through our daughter's veins was more than Beth could handle without a reaction, and I held her as she cried for a second time that day.

Sam's response to the influx of chemo was nearly instantaneous. More nausea and a feeling of uneasiness gripped her, and she begged to leave every few minutes. Once the chemo infusion was done, and she'd been given another saline flush, we were finally able to leave and start making our way back home. We'd only driven about five minutes when Sam started dry heaving in the backseat, and she announced she didn't want to go back and do that again. I just kept thanking God for how smoothly that day had gone and told myself, "One down, only eleven more to go."

## Chapter Eight

# Divine

I HAVE THIS IMAGE in my mind—perhaps you envision a similar one from time to time. God and I are walking along a picturesque path, strolling on the ocean shore with the soothing sound of waves in the background. No words are exchanged, yet I feel the kind of comfort I find only in the company of an intimate friend.

Then far in the distance, I notice a storm brewing over the depths of the ocean. At first, I only see it out of the corner of my eye, but then a roll of thunder ripples through the air, and I redirect my focus from where I am to where I could be. Radiant fingerlings of lightning flash violently across the sky, and the thunder rumbles more loudly. For those of us with an affinity for intensity, the desire to drift closer to the storm creates a pang deep within us. We may not want to venture into the fiercest part of the tempest and risk total destruction, but the craving to feel the heat of the lightning bolts exerts a gravitational pull over us. Then I remember God. He hasn't continued walking along the shore without me; He's still standing only a foot away, watching me as I watch the storm. In His eyes I can see both understanding and concern. He knows that I want to go, even if only for a moment, but He wonders why I would put myself in harm's way for a cheap thrill or even a rush of adrenaline. Despite His proximity, I remind myself that He isn't going anywhere, that a quick trip into the water will be over almost as soon as it begins, and that He's the one responsible for my wiring, so He understands. In my vision, He watches from the beach as I dive under the waves to swim out in the open ocean.

I'd like to pretend that most of my sins are spontaneous, happening in the blink of an eye when I don't notice or know any better. But the reality of most of my spiritual struggles is that they aren't accidents; they're premeditated, well-thought-out rationalizations. I'm fortunate enough to be in God's presence, undistracted by the white noise of life, and my focus on our relationship is pure. Then my eye catches the glimmer of distant lightning. I know the damage that a lightning strike causes; I've seen the live newsfeeds of forest fires, charred remnants of homes, and the occasional loss of life from a direct hit. When I was younger, the thunder first scared then startled me; but eventually, I felt no effect at all, no matter how loud or how close it got. The same goes for the lightning; its power once seemed threatening, but in time, it became more like an exciting friend I was only able to see up close and personal on rare occasions. So when a bolt bursts from nothingness and thunder ripples through the clouds, I'm instinctively drawn in.

When storms roll across the sky in Houston, they typically start in the west and spread eastward across the city. From my vantage point, driving to and from work along Interstate 59, I can watch the clouds gather on the horizon, knowing they will make their way to my doorstep a few hours later. If I were focused on safety, seeing the storm coming would give me time to batten down the hatches before the first drop of rain arrived. Instead, I'm the type who waits for the most intense part of the storm, then steps outside to feel the rain soaking through my clothes and the wind wrapping around me. I enjoy the tangible, tactile experience of it all.

Growing up in a Baptist environment, sin was portrayed as a scary thing. The God of the Old Testament takes center stage, with allusions to destruction, oppression, and violent discipline if His people let sin blow its way into their lives. As I aged, my perspective changed, and the focus on the forgiveness and grace of the New Testament replaced my childhood fears of retribution. Right or wrong, I started to see Jesus as an evolution of God, something like Divinity 2.0, with more compassion, less intensity, and a far greater understanding of what it was really like to be human. With that new lens, sin didn't seem quite so heinous an offense. It wasn't because the nature of sin itself had changed but because the threat of punishment had lessened in intensity.

With that kind of perspective, the rationalization of sin flourishes rapidly. If forgiveness is less than a breath away, the sin I have in mind isn't going to do anyone harm, and it may even remind me of why it's important not to sin. A little step closer to the lightning isn't such a bad thing, is it?

But just like the initial fear I felt of lightning and thunder, the closer I get to sin, the less dangerous it appears. And with more close calls and no catastrophic results, it almost seems safe to stand in the middle of the storm. There's just one problem: a direct hit would still annihilate me. I lose sight of that and, in my hubris, either see sin as less than sin or elevate myself to a plane where I am more immune to its toxicity than others. It may not be self-deification, but it's not far off. I can even convince myself that if the rain is falling intensely enough, I'll be obscured in a shadow or tucked so far behind the waves that even God, from His resting place on the shore, won't notice what I'm doing. Once I've had my fill, I'll swim back, take up my walk by His side, and act as if nothing ever happened. As with many lessons over the last year and a half, my perspective changed one afternoon, this time following one of Samantha's weekly chemo sessions.

As I've already mentioned, those infusions were intense and draining on many levels. Shortly after the IVs started, she felt edgy, restless, and wanted to get up to move around. Then, usually right before we finished for the day, a metallic taste would coat her mouth, leaving her alternately disinterested in food and violently resistant to even the smell of it. Without fail, at some point along the drive home, she'd start retching, her body attempting to reject food she'd not consumed. By the time we gathered Noah and we made it to the house, which was usually 4:00 p.m., the 'roid rage from the drugs was in full effect. She was faster, more aggressive, and perpetually in motion. One of the safest ways to get her to burn off some of that steam was to take her on bike rides. While we were cautious about her activity level and tried to keep her subdued to ensure no infections crept in while she was on chemo, she needed an outlet for her energy, or she would lie awake, moving restlessly all night.

After Sam's fourth infusion, Beth decided to take her for a ride when I went to get Noah from a friend's house. While Samantha rode her bike, Beth ran behind her to pace her and be ready to catch her if she fell. The usual ride that Sam did was a little north of two miles on the greenbelt trail near our house. The journey would start with the girls making their way along the outskirts of a man-made lake before moving onto a paved path through the woods. The trail was a wide ellipse, with periodic tangents offering ways to get to other greenbelt trails or elongate the route they were on. During these post-treatment workouts, Beth had to be extremely patient because she never knew what Sam's mood might be. There were some days where Sam hardly made it down the street before exhaustion eclipsed the steroids, and she broke down in tears, entirely devoid of the energy to go on. Other days, she was unstoppable, riding on for miles, growing enraged at the prospect of heading back to the house. On that particular afternoon, Sam was vacillating between exhausted and energetic as Beth jogged behind her to wait and see which version of our daughter would rule the day.

After nearly a mile and a half, the girls came to a fork in the road. One path led back to the house; another moved away from it, increasing the distance from two to three miles in all. Just before that fork, Samantha stopped pedaling and came to a halt where the two paths diverged. With a blend of annoyance and anger, she turned to Beth.

"Which path are we going to take?" Samantha asked.

"You can choose whichever one you want," replied Beth in a measured, cautious tone.

"I don't know, just pick one, and tell me which way to go," Samantha said with annoyance in her voice.

"Why don't we—" Beth began, before being interrupted by Sam shouting, "And whichever way you choose, I'm going the other direction!"

"To the right," Beth called.

Beth watched, teeth gritted, as Sam's feet found the pedals, started moving, and directed her bike down the path on the left. Despite her illness, outbursts like this were still not well received in our house. Parents are to be respected even when circumstances are less than desirable, and discipline isn't something that's often withheld when that line is crossed. However, in this instance, while Beth's natural instinct urged her to address Sam's rebellion, her compassion led her in another direction. As Samantha peddled onward, choosing the path Beth hadn't picked for her, Beth didn't just stand there waiting for the prodigal child to return; she counted to ten and started jogging along behind her again.

All this time, I'd envisioned God standing on the shoreline watching from afar as I swam alone in the depths of the ocean, flirting with the tempest around me. But that's not the way God works. It's just the way I want Him to work so I can have the freedom to self-indulge from a distance.

No matter how far out I go, no matter how violent the storm I choose to swim into, He's there, right behind me. When I view God as an active participant in my life during those times, His face only inches away from the harm I'm doing myself, it places a profound burden on my heart. Beth wanted to lash out, to discipline a wayward, rebellious child, but she didn't. She ran within reach, through moments of frustration and disappointment, eternally ready to reach out a loving hand to catch her child if ever she fell.

# Chapter Nine

# Eye of the Storm

WITH INFUSIONS ALREADY under way, I turned my attention to the next obstacle in Sam's diagnosis and treatment plan, the MRI. The afternoon before that appointment, I got a call from the radiology team. Due to a schedule conflict the next day, there would be no sedation team available by the time Sam wrapped up infusions and got to the radiology floor. We had to either reschedule the appointment for the next week or have the MRI with no option for chemical assistance to take the edge off if things got ugly.

We were already going for the majority of a day once a week and felt that Sam was enduring enough time away from her friends at school, so we didn't want to reschedule. During the conversation on the phone, rheumatology was patched in to join the discussion and arrive at a decision. In the end, they'd told me that since it was only on her leg, she wouldn't have to go all the way into the machine, there'd be no need for contrast (which would have doubled the time required for the imaging), and it should only take about twenty minutes all-in. There was always the option of giving it a try and rescheduling to do it with sedation a few days later if it didn't go well. With all of that in mind, we agreed to have the MRI, sans sedation, so we could finally get a sense of just how invasive the next steps in her treatment plan were going to be.

The following day went as most of her previous weekly trips had; she'd go to school for the first few hours of the day, and I'd collect her around ten thirty in the morning to drive into town for a twelve o'clock appointment. By that time, she was a pro at the infusions. She'd pack a ladybug-shaped suitcase with some essentials: her stuffed animal named Muscal, an iPod given to her by a slew of friends from church, the weekly barrage of get-well cards I will mention later, at least one copy of the Bible, a handful of books, and a few random items she'd chosen that morning. The IVs were run-of-the-mill as well: an hour and a half of steroids, a ten-minute saline flush, fifteen minutes of chemo, and another flush of saline.

By the time we got up to radiology, it was pretty late in the afternoon. The patients were thinning out; the staff was definitely ready to head home, and Samantha was feeling the less-than-desirable effects of her medications. Paperwork took a solid twenty minutes to complete, followed by conversations with the technicians to get a lay of the land before heading in. While in the waiting area, we saw a ten-year-old boy, with a brace on his wrist, who was coming out of sedation a few beds down. He was confused, incoherent, and alternately crying and falling asleep sitting up. Samantha was watching him closely, so I explained that he had been given medicine to keep him still during the MRI. I told her that kind of reaction to the drugs was exactly what I was trying to avoid by choosing not to sedate her as well. She understood the logic of my words, but I could still sense her apprehension and growing discomfort with the idea of what was to come. Her unasked question hovered in the air: *What was so bad that it required knocking kids out with drugs so that they could endure it?*

Once we finally made it back to the room, the techs were great. They had a special set of headphones and goggles rigged up so that Sam could watch a movie during the MRI. This was a brilliant distraction technique to keep the kids from realizing they were inside a tube with only inches of clearance above their faces. It was also designed to drown out the "construction zone" sounds the machine would make every few minutes once it was operating. The concept was easy enough: lie down on a table, ignore some noise while you're watching a movie, and it's all over before the closing credits roll.

While we always encourage physical activity in our house, it came back to bite us in this particular instance. Samantha hates sitting still and never watches TV, so what would have been a treat for some kids was closer to cruel and unusual punishment for her. I tried to get her interested in a couple of CDs and movies I'd brought, but she was busy staring at the monstrosity of a machine in front of her, taking the entire room in before she said a word or moved a muscle. The room was smaller than I'd expected, about the size of our family room at home. In the center sat the MRI machine, which spanned floor to ceiling and half the width of the space. The circular aperture in the center was like a perfect metallic doughnut, save the table and track running through the lower aspect of the contraption. Along the wall were blankets, vests, and other accoutrements, but her focus was clearly on the overwhelming stature of the structure itself. The technician made Samantha so comfortable that it was surprisingly easy to get her to climb onto the table and start getting her ready. I attempted to sell Sam on the headphones and goggles, both of which she declined because she wanted to be able to see what was happening. I did manage to talk her into accepting some earplugs to help deaden the sounds, but it was clear from the expression on the tech's face that those wouldn't be anywhere near enough on their own. After that, the tech arranged a baluster and a series of straps, which were necessary to keep Sam's leg perfectly still since the images would be ruined by the slightest movement. Samantha was hesitant but agreeable, so within fifteen minutes of entering the room, she was on the table with her lower body strapped into place and ready to go. I was talking to her, making jokes, and holding her hand, but the moment of truth was yet to come.

With Sam's hand still in mine, the tech pressed a button on the machine, and the table slid horizontally along its track, inching slowly toward the opening. First her toes slid in, then her knee, her waist, and a moment later, her eyes lost sight of mine as her head slipped out of view. The instant she could no longer see me, the composure she'd maintained up until that moment toppled like a house of cards, and she started screaming and thrashing, pleading to be taken back out.

The movement of the table was reversed, and Samantha's face drifted back into view, tears welling up in her eyes and sitting up to hug me the moment she had enough room to reach me. Whoever felt she wouldn't have to go all the way in the tube must have thought she was Wilt Chamberlain, not a six-year-old girl with parents whose stature leaves eligibility to ride roller coasters questionable at times. After a brief conversation, the tech apologized for what I was told on the phone but assured me that the position of the camera required Samantha being fully in the tube. Samantha pleaded not to be put back in and tore at the straps holding her lower body in place, but I was able to calm her down a bit. Her request—I'll rephrase that, her demand—in exchange for her cooperation was simple: she wanted to be able to see me. She told me that as long as she could see me, she would be brave enough to do it, and it was only once she lost sight of me that fear took hold.

At that point, a second tech came into the room, and we adults started to converse about how to make things work. If she were lying in the opposite direction so that her head was where her feet had been, it would add a few inches to her field of vision so she'd have a glimpse of me, which I ruled out because she'd have to be fed through the tube to get there. They tried getting her to focus on the movie playing on the high-tech goggles, but she wasn't budging on the idea of losing visibility. They recommended calling it off and coming back later, but Samantha didn't want to be sedated (after seeing what it looked like to come out of it), and I wasn't a fan of pumping more meds into her either. The solution came as her tiny voice posed a question, "What if I lie on my stomach? Then I can look out of the tube, and see you the whole time, right?" We all stared at one another for a moment before one tech shook his head no, but clearly out of skepticism, not certainty. At that point, my patience may have been a bit thin, and my comment to his reaction might have been something akin to, "It's a picture that you're taking in a circle, if she's flipped over, just read the film upside down. There's no reason that shouldn't work, go call someone to confirm." He sidled out of the room and returned a few moments later to announce that lying on her stomach was theoretically fine but that it would be harder for her to remain perfectly still in that position, and it might take longer than expected if the pictures had to be retaken.

The fetters on her legs were removed, her posture reversed, and everything was reapplied to arrange her body facing down. When the time came for her to be moved back into the tube, I could see her tensing. Ignoring the glare from the tech that remained in the room, I climbed onto the table with her. I pressed my lips to her ear and whispered, "I promise, this isn't going to hurt you. I'm right here with you, and I love you." I said it over and over as the table migrated into the tube, knowing that, in a moment, the sounds of the machine would blast my voice away. I only hoped that she'd remember my words in the midst of the cacophony to come.

The first round of vibrations and sounds was more intense than expected, and I felt her body recoil, which was met with a chastising voice coming through a nearby speaker. "She moved, so we'll have to take that one again." The next set of sounds was anticipated, so she didn't flinch; instead, her reaction was to silently sob as we remained pressed together. I could feel the agony of her fear and her internal pleading to be anywhere but where she was right then.

Lying cheek to cheek in the eye of the storm, her fear and my concern collided. Twin rivulets of warm tears trickled down to the bed of the MRI; our hearts cried out as one in the silence. "Father, why have you forsaken me?" Her cry to me, my cry to Him, then the jackhammerlike pounding of the machine began anew.

The first few rounds of images were the worst; the unexpectedness of it all had taken us both aback, and we were struggling to regain our footing. But in time, she knew when the noises were coming, how to shift around between images to help her stay still when they took the next picture, and she even grew comfortable enough for me to slip back a few inches so we could look at each other to talk. As we pressed toward forty-five minutes in the machine, her patience was waning, but the voice in the speaker announced that there were only two pictures left to take, so it was almost over. Just over an hour after we'd gone in, we emerged hand in hand, skipping down the hallway, singing to celebrate conquering her fear, and rejoicing that the day that began six hours earlier was finally drawing to a close.

How was I to process that day, her agony, and what good could possibly come from it? Particularly if the MRI results came back as her doctor and I expected, leading us further down a path of treatment that would be far more invasive and terrifying than an IV of chemo.

It was months before I was able to reflect on that experience with a clear mind. It had, unarguably, been one of my hardest hours as a father—though that too would change over the year and a half to follow. My innate reaction to anything that threatens those that I love is to eradicate it—temporarily, permanently, in any way I must—to ease their suffering. I would willingly endure any degree of pain myself if it meant they didn't have to but that wasn't an option in this instance. Perhaps because I was unable to do that, I had to find other ways to cope with the suffering and see it in a different light.

In that room, I was so busy focusing on the pain of the moment that I lost sight of the healing it was meant to bring. The sort of inward look the MRI would accomplish mirrored a degree of introspection that I so often don't have. I don't want to sit still and look beneath the surface typically because I already know how messed up everything under there is, and bringing it into focus is a painful process. But if

EYE OF THE STORM

we're to be healed, if we're to truly find the root of our anger, bitterness, dissatisfaction, unhappiness, and other struggles, it sometimes means we must endure temporal pains to attain eternal glory.

I also think God whispers to me constantly in the way I whispered to her. "I'm here. I'll protect you. I know that this may scare you, but it isn't going to break you." He calls to me as He called to Peter, telling me to walk with Him on the surface of the sea in the middle of a storm. But like the disciple, my gaze wanders, and the water instantly engulfs me. If only I kept my eyes on Him and remained unafraid—if only.

# Chapter Ten

# Abide in Me

WHAT WAS TAKING so long? The tech from radiology said that the images would be available the next morning, that the doctor would have them right afterward, and that I should get a call about how things looked by early afternoon.

As time pressed on and the silence grew louder, my mind kept playing image after image in a continuous loop. I already don't sleep much, so I know that after a couple of days with little to no sleep, I start to reach a breaking point where the tapestry of reality begins to unravel. The cycle of time that keeps me in check grows distorted, and eight hours of darkness can seem to drag on for days.

Hours turned into days, days into nights, and with each revolution of dawn and dusk, sleep remained elusive. On the fourth night without sleep, God chose to make His voice heard. His whisper resonated through my mind, "Abide in Me."

Those words struck a chord in my memory because of an ambitious undertaking Beth had a couple of years earlier. In a young moms' Bible study she was attending, they were challenged to memorize John 15:1–17 in its entirety. That's 354 words, spanning twenty lines of scripture—needless to say, quite a task. Every night, after she read over an increasingly large stack of index cards with one verse on each, she would recite it aloud so I could make sure she'd gotten it right. In the midst of those verses is this one, spoken by Jesus, "I am the vine; you are the branches. If you remain in me and I in you, you will bear much fruit; apart from me you can do nothing." A few verses later comes this explanation for why we are to abide in Him. "I have told you this so that my joy may be in you and that your joy may be complete." At this point, to say that joy isn't exactly at the forefront of my mind would be something of an understatement, so I'll express my reaction to that whisper as best as I can.

For the men out there, you've no doubt experienced something like the picture I'm about to paint. You've been busy at work for the day, perhaps daydreaming during meetings, thinking of spending some long-overdue time with your wife to reconnect. You play out the scenario for the evening, and by the time you pull into the garage, you know exactly how things are going to go over the course of the next few hours. Then you open the back door and step into the house.

The scene before you looks a bit like a clip from a bad movie on parenting. The game room is a complete and total disaster, littered with backpacks, untouched pages of homework, and a pile of shoes that comes up to your knees. Your wife is visible in the kitchen with all four burners on the stove going, and you're met with an aroma that indicates things clearly aren't going well on at least one of them. You make a mental note of where the fire extinguisher is tucked away, just in case. On your way into the kitchen, you have to sidestep your two children as they run past you at full throttle, screaming at each other and collectively wearing one T-shirt and a pair of socks. As you step closer to your blushing bride, you notice her hair is a bit askew, then you realize that there's no hair tie keeping it in place. It's an amalgam of oils and sweat holding it in a quasi-ponytail, meaning she's likely not washed it in at least two days. Your mind connects the dots that if she hasn't washed her hair in two days, her legs probably feel a bit like a short-haired wookie, but you're not about to let that slow your roll.

Into the kitchen you stroll, dropping an elbow onto the counter, and in your most alluring voice you ask, "How you doin'?"

Now, if you've done this before, you probably just reflexively covered your vital organs because you know what's coming. Before turning around, she rises to her full height, takes a deep breath, extends and relaxes her fingers so they no longer look like she's strangling the countertop, and turns to face you—at which point, she lets loose.

"You've got to be kidding me, you're thinking about that now? Do you not see what's going on around here? Can you not tell that I'm completely underwater, and that I can't even start to see how to get all of this under control? Why don't you figure out what your kids are screaming about? Better yet, can you tell me why they are pretty much naked? Oh, that's right, the laundry isn't done yet. And if I remember correctly, the reason it isn't done yet is because you haven't fixed the washer that broke two weeks ago. Do you know what it's like to manually agitate a washing machine for two weeks? How about you fix some of what's broken around here and then I can think about doing what you want?"

Once she's finished saying all of that, you opt not to respond with what came to mind, "So is that a firm no, or is there some wiggle room there?" You may have had a plan in mind, but she's clearly not in a mood to entertain it.

After four days without sleep, I was struggling with the growing expectation that the MRI would show a need for surgery. I also knew that even surgery may not ward off a permanent physical disability for my daughter when God stepped through the chaos, strolled into the kitchen, and whispered, "Abide in Me," and I let loose.

My response to Him mirrored her response to me. Now, in this condition, with everything that's broken, with you not fixing things I know you're capable of fixing? You've got to be kidding me. How about you do your part and then I'll consider doing mine?

I have no doubt that my little tirade caused some wide-eyed glares from the angels that were listening in, but the call from Him remained the same. It was simple, unrelenting, and devoid of judgment for my unwillingness to fully put my faith in Him up until that moment. Confused and concerned, but undoubtedly called, I did the only thing that you can do when the place in which you find yourself seems to be light-years away from the place He wants you to go: I started praying. No fancy words, no verses to quote, just an internal dialogue between the broken and the divine.

After a few minutes of prayer, I opened my eyes and noticed something was wrong; faint purple light was streaming in through the gossamer curtains of the bedroom window. I turned to look at the clock and realized it had been nearly four hours since I'd started praying. Somewhere in the midst of my conversation with God, I'd drifted into a dreamless sleep.

I won't claim that I awoke enveloped with a sense of joy, but for the first time in two months, I found myself unafraid for my daughter's well-being. It was in that moment that I accepted the uncertainty of what was to come and felt confident that, no matter what the outcome, I would find a way to set my instinctive reactions aside and abide in Him.

Up until that night, I'd been so singularly focused on completely healing her that I had failed to see all of the ways people were trying to bring joy into Samantha's life. I had fallen prey to exactly what Joseph Bayly wrote to avoid at all costs, "Do not forget in the darkness what you learned in the light." When my eyes opened that morning, and dawn slowly bled into the room, I saw things with a luminance that only comes from above.

# Chapter Eleven

# New Eyes

Date: Tuesday, 18 October 2011
Subject: Samantha

We wanted to give everyone an update on how Sam is doing.

As far as infusions go, we have another trip to Texas Children's tomorrow for steroids and to have a nurse teach us how to give her methotrexate shots at home. After that tutorial, we'll actually give her the first shot tomorrow, which we expect to be doing weekly for at least a year. As for the steroid, we're going to go back to the hospital a few more times over the next month to get infusions, but then we'll be done with steroids for good. While we had hoped to be finished with hospital trips after tomorrow's visit, the prospect of avoiding 'roid rage for the next year (we thought we'd have to do weekly shots of that at home as well) is definitely a welcomed relief!

Sam is still handling the treatments really well despite the nausea and restlessness after each round. She's gotten along so well with the nurses in the infusion center that (after they put in the IV) they actually let her work the syringe to draw her own blood and push her own saline flush last time around, which she thought was very cool. She's definitely ready for this to be over with and to have a normal schedule again, but she's been incredibly tough through it all. We're so proud of her!

On a final note, we got the MRI results back from the doctor, and it looks like there are no areas of active inflammation in her bones or muscles, which is the best outcome we could have hoped for. The doctor said that the reason it took so long to get us a final verdict is because he kept having other doctors and radiologists review the MRI images since he expected some degree of bone/muscle involvement based on how extensive the patch of morphea on her leg is. In conveying the results, he was using words like "amazing" and "unexplainable" to convey his surprise at just how good the internal images are.

From a medical perspective, she shouldn't already have visible improvement in her skin tissue, she shouldn't be unaffected in her mobility, and she shouldn't be untouched beneath the superficial layers we can see. While the doctors may not be able to articulate why her results seem to defy their expectations, the explanation is painfully obvious to us. So many people interceding on her behalf through fervent prayer for her health, happiness, and faith during this struggle has had an impact that transcends what science and statistics alone can explain. As parents of a little girl who had the potential to be physically disabled as a result of this disease, we can't thank you enough for all that you've done for her. Our hearts have been forever touched by the hand of God, moving through all of you.

Love you!
Beth and Chris

"HOW CAN WE help?" It was a question I'd heard at least a few dozen times a week, and each time, my answer was roughly the same. "Actually, we're doing pretty well, all things considered. Aside from prayer, there's not really anything we need, but it's very thoughtful of you to ask." Why no one looked me in the eyes and said "BS" was simply an act of compassion and not wanting to expose my emotional frailty. Again, I was so absorbed with remedying the specific problem Samantha had that I ignored the majority of the world around me.

In the light of day, after the abide-in-me epiphany, I found that the outpouring of unsolicited support for my family was overwhelming. Not a single infusion day went by where we didn't have a warm meal arrive at dinnertime. Within two weeks of Sam's first chemo treatment, an iPod and iTunes gift card showed up on our doorstep, a gift from the parents of her friends in Sunday school who wanted to help her pass the hours she spent getting IVs. While we were incredibly grateful for the things everyone was doing, we weren't actually asking anyone for help.

It was then that I remembered a passage from Don Piper's book *90 Minutes in Heaven* where a friend of his comes to visit him in the hospital after a horrific accident that took his life for an hour and a half, thus the title. Members of Don's congregation kept showing up at the hospital asking how they could help, and he, being their shepherd, found it impossible to yield to their requests and let them take care of him. This friend of his finally came in, sat down, and called BS on what he was doing, branding it as selfishness, not strength. Pride, particularly as men who have it all figured out, can be a vicious enemy to accepting the gifts others come offering for our benefit. Admitting that you want, much less need, help somehow exposes a weakness that you don't want others to know exists. In retrospect, their offers to help were the only way people knew how to show their concern and express their love. Then I realized that they were trying to show their love for her, not for me. All this time, I'd been pushing them away because I didn't need help, completely blind to the fact that it wasn't actually me they were reaching out to embrace through their actions. For those of you reading this who offered to help, I sincerely apologize for not being man enough to accept your assistance sooner. It's so easy in our culture to avoid admitting our shortcomings that we fail to find the strength to take hold of a hand outstretched in compassion. Once I started to search for the joy surrounding me, I saw that I'd been depriving my ailing daughter the most joyous thing in existence, the love of others.

From then on, when people asked what they could do, I found some way to take them up on the offer to help. At times, it was as simple as needing something done around the house or help watching Noah while Sam was getting treatments. When people at the office wanted to pitch in, I told them I didn't need any assistance at work per se, but I noticed that the infusion center was wildly understocked on books, movies, and toys. By the end of the week, my trunk and backseat were at capacity with everything from blankets to board games to books to boxes of movies, including *The Exorcist* (someone was clearly just dumping out every VHS they owned), which I opted to pull out before going to the hospital. After all, the kids there already had enough to handle without seeing someone's head spin around in circles.

The most beautiful display of love, however, arrives in our mailbox on Tuesday evenings. To help pass the time in the infusion center, we'd asked some of Samantha's friends to send her notes, drawings, mazes, and word search puzzles she could go through in the hospital. I was expecting three or four letters a week to keep her busy, which would have been awesome. It turns out that I wildly underestimated the lengths her friends would go to in an effort to show their love for her. Week by week, the mailbox grew more inundated, and gathering Sam's fan mail became something of a family effort. We would walk out, each grasp a handful, and bring them inside to sort through the stack before packing them to take with her the next day. Some of Sam's friends even sent Noah letters to be sure he didn't feel left out, which he absolutely loved.

After reading through them during her IVs and playing games the kids had made up, we would put the stack back into her suitcase to bring them home. Those were sacred gifts, and we wanted to hold on to them, but we weren't quite sure what to do with them at first. Since we wanted Sam to see how much people loved her, we ultimately decided to start taping the letters to the bottom of a wall in her room. Since she's a bit persnickety and will only sleep facing one direction, we put them on the wall that was always in her field of vision so she could fall asleep (or lie awake after steroids) looking at them. As the weeks passed, what began as a single strip on the bottom of her wall grew into a latticework of paper that covered every inch on that side of her room, floor to ceiling. There were times when she was outside playing or preoccupied with some new project, and I would just sit there, staring at that wall, thanking each of them for their compassion.

Had I not been strong enough to ask for help, I would have continued to deprive my little girl of that outpouring of love. She never would have received all those letters, never would have felt the warmth of their affection, and never would have had that beautiful view in her room to ease her to sleep every night.

# Chapter Twelve

# Final Infusion

I F WE FOLLOWED our routine appointment schedule, Samantha would have been in the hospital for her final round of infusions on her seventh birthday. We decided to move her appointment to a different day to allow some modicum of celebration despite the circumstances. Since she was on chemo, and exposure to other kids was a problem, we weren't able to have a traditional birthday party with a slew of her friends, so we opted to let her invite over a single friend and take them on a mini shopping spree. As we watched Sam, her friend, and Noah peruse one store after another, I couldn't help but periodically remember that the end of her IVs meant the start of a new chapter in her treatments.

We were going to be done with steroids completely, which was a huge blessing, considering how edgy, restless, and uneasy they made her. Wrapping up infusions wasn't the end of chemo, however; it was the beginning of at-home injections. The dosage would drop to 0.6 milliliters a week, far less than her infusions, but the method of getting the drug into her system wasn't going to be fun. To give chemo injections, the medication has to go directly into a spot where there's excess skin. For plenty of kids, that's not an issue, but my daughter is the only seven-year-old I've ever seen with an eight-pack, meaning pockets of extra skin are few and far between. When the doctor said that transitioning to injections at the house meant the shots would have to go into the skin of her stomach, I instantly had concerns about how uncomfortable that would be. Hypothetically speaking, had I injected myself with a few syringes of chemo, I'd be able to say how caustic it is and how you quickly get a sense of nausea once it's in your system. That's hypothetical, of course, someone would have to be nuts to inject himself with chemo just to understand how his daughter felt, right? Along with the physical discomfort and nausea, there's the psychological trauma of a needle going into your stomach. There are people who look away and pretend a shot isn't coming, but Sam watched the needle go in every time during her IVs, and the chemo injections in her stomach would be no different.

With respect to who would be handling the shots at the house, there was no question in my mind about where that responsibility fell. This was another path I wasn't going to let Beth traverse; I wouldn't let her touch one of those needles or force her to look into Samantha's eyes the split-second after an injection. I wouldn't allow that suffering for her, and barring something that physically disables me, she'll never know the feeling I have right now. She can play the bad guy when it comes to forcing reading, cleaning, and general hygiene, but not when it comes to this.

I push past the momentary loss of focus and back into the moment God has placed before me; my daughter's sunken eyes bright with delight as she joins in a dance routine with her friend, my son applauding the performance, and my wife enjoying a rare moment where worry isn't weighing her down. While there may be instances when looking into the future creates hope or carries me to a happier place, I usually find that it simply creates burdens I'm not meant to carry. I wonder how frequently God wishes we'd be exactly where we are; my guess is, He hopes that in every moment of our existence. Psalm 46:10 reminds us to "be still and know that I am God." I'm always so busy racing to the next moment, confronting the next battle, or sizing up the next obstacle that I often fail to fully experience the depth of what today affords me.

On the day of her final round of IVs, I stopped thinking about the long road ahead and how hard it might be on all of us. I spent every moment only in the room where I sat and didn't dilute how much of myself I gave to my wife and daughter as we passed those hours together. It was during that final trip that I realized how many games we'd played together, how many ridiculous stories we'd made up to pass the time, and how we could feel the gravity of the love we were all expressing from one moment to the next. I never thought I'd be sad to lose that time, but how often do men in corporate America afford themselves the opportunity to spend one workday a week doing nothing but caring for their wives and children? I know that in the months since, my days have been spent in an office and, while I'd never want to go through any of it again, part of me misses the bonds built during those months in the infusion center.

Perhaps a novel idea would be to experience moments like that in the absence of some crisis. Maybe I should try setting aside the to-do lists, backlog of work, and schedule-filling activities and just be still wherever I am. I find that in the rare instances that I'm truly focused on my friends, family, or even the simplicity of the beautifully constructed world around me, God is always there waiting with open arms to make my joy complete.

# Chapter Thirteen

# Warrior

Date: Friday, 2 March 2012
Subject: BBE Early Act First Knight Award
CONFIDENTIAL

Dear Parents of Samantha Slaughter,

The students and staff at Bear Branch Elementary School in partnership with the Kingwood Rotarians began an exciting character development program on September 12, 2011. The Early Act First Knight curriculum encourages students to live according to a modern code of chivalry. The EAFK knight, Sir Cass, and Kingwood Rotarians will be at BBE **Wednesday, March 7th,** to award EAFK medals to a student in every classroom, each selected by the teacher, who best exemplifies the character virtue that has been taught during the previous month. This past month the students focused on the virtue of **Perseverance**. Samantha has been selected to become knighted. Your presence is requested as we honor your child. At the ceremony your child will be led by our knights in armor as they are called to the stage to receive beautiful medallions and the rankings of Page, Squire, or Knight. The student's family will be invited to join him or her onstage. After receiving the medal your child will take a seat on stage in the "Gallery of Champions."

Our students will not know who has been selected to be knighted from the class until the name is called. **Please help us to build the suspense by keeping this information confidential.**

S AM'S BEEN A fighter since she developed the ability to move, which started before she took her first breath. During the second trimester of Beth's pregnancy, she would take an internal beating at 1:00 a.m. on a nightly basis. Samantha was hungry, so she'd start with gentle shoves, then work her way into a full-on boxing match in the womb until Beth got up and ate a huge bowl of cereal. Within ten minutes, Sam's hunger sated, she'd calm down and slide back into motionlessness. When she was born, three weeks early via C-section because of a prolapsed umbilical cord, she came out kicking and screaming.

As a newborn, things were no different. She had colic, and for two hours a night, typically from one to three in the morning, she'd just scream, and there was no way to stop her. People recommended car rides, which she hated. Some said to put her on the dryer with it turned on, which didn't help either. Swings, swaddles, songs, and snuggling were all useless. The only thing that remotely worked was to push her around the house in her stroller and periodically bump into door frames (discovered on accident while nearly sleepwalking one night), but even that didn't do the trick for long.

As an infant, Beth took her to a friend's house, and Samantha scared a dog back into its kennel. As she crawled around to take in her new surroundings in the house, the unexpected canine rounded a corner and took Sam by surprise. Instead of crying and running away, Sam puffed herself up like an angry cat, started screaming, and crawled toward the dog until it went into hiding. There was the day when she was two, and she laid out a four-year-old twice her size when the girl tried to steal her snack (are you noticing a theme around food yet?), the time in kindergarten that she picked up a boy who was knocking down one of her friends and literally tossed him off of the playground, and the list goes on. My favorite memory, though, was when she decided to retaliate after Beth gave her one of her first spankings.

Samantha was eight months old, incredibly active and strong willed. When it came time to change her diaper, there was often a minor skirmish because she wouldn't want to stop playing. From time to time, the fight escalated beyond cries, and she would express her frustration in a physical fashion. One day, Beth picked Sam up, set her on the changing table, and leaned in to take off her dirty diaper. As Beth leaned forward, Samantha cocked back a leg and kicked as hard as she could. Normally, it wouldn't be too big of a deal, but given the angle Beth used for her approach, the kick landed in the middle of her C-section scar. The scar had healed well, and Beth had been back to running as soon as she was able, but direct contact with that spot was still painful for her. When Samantha landed that kick, Beth reacted with a swift and firm swat to Sam's exposed thigh. This is the point where most children scream and cry because of the pain, but not Sam; she just glared at Beth as if some unseen line had been crossed. Beth saw the wheels turning in Sam's mind and, thinking she had enlightened her infant daughter on child-parent positions of authority, leaned in once more to finish changing the diaper. Samantha kicked with the same ferocity and hit the exact same spot. As Beth's hand flew downward to swat Samantha's thigh, Sam's outstretched index finger raced upward, finding its mark dead center in Beth's eye. Clearly an Old Testament scholar at eight months of age, Samantha heeded the directive in Exodus and took an eye for a thigh. It's Bible humor, work with me, people!

At the onset of her illness, once I knew that there was a high likelihood of her being physically disabled, my greatest concern wasn't aesthetic. Of course, I knew there would be hardships; we can be especially venomous toward each other as human beings, particularly when it comes to someone who doesn't look the right way. I fully expected tear-filled nights, a growing degree of introversion, and a focus on activities where her disability would be less obvious. More than any of that, though, I was concerned that some aspect of who she was would change over the course of her disease. I was afraid she would lose some facet of the strength that had defined her even in the womb; but on March 7, 2012, that fear was put to rest, and it hasn't resurfaced since.

Samantha's school is one of a handful in the Houston area that participates in a program called the Early Act First Knight, which is run by the local Rotary Club. As part of this program, during morning announcements, the kids in the school are reminded of the attributes they should strive to exemplify and get guidance on how to make good choices throughout the day. To help reinforce that concept, the students learn about one character attribute every month—things like compassion, tolerance, honesty, service, and others. As a culmination of that month's learning, the teacher of each class chooses the student that best exemplifies the attribute they've been studying, and that child receives an award. The award, however, is much more than a gold star on the chore chart. First of all, the recipient's identities are kept a secret. No one but the teacher knows who has won until an award ceremony takes place. In the days leading up to the event, we would hear the kids talking about who should win because so-and-so was the most thoughtful or respectful, which is an incredible thing for a parent to hear seven-year-olds recognizing and discussing.

The ceremony itself takes the concept of awards to another level entirely. At Samantha's school, they bring all of the kindergarten, first-grade, and second-grade students into the cafeteria in the morning; third, fourth, and fifth grade repeat the process later in the day. Once inside, they are met by a pair of men dressed in full knight regalia: swords, chain mail, coats of arms—the works. The knights pump the crowd up with outlandish tales of courage and heroism, so the kids are literally trembling with excitement when the first teacher walks up to the stage to announce the winner for their class. The kids sit with crossed legs and joined hands as each class's teacher reads a one-page accolade about the student that emulates the quality they've been studying, and at the very end of her speech, she announces the name of the child. The kids erupt with applause and cheers, and music boosted from the *Braveheart* soundtrack roars into life as the winner ascends the stairs to meet one of the knights, who places a medallion around the kid's neck. As the child walks up, his or her parents, who have been tucked away behind stage, step into view; everyone hugs, and most of the men choke back tears of pride. After that, the kids are escorted over to the "Gallery of Champions" on the side of the stage and sit to bask in the envy of their classmates until all of the awards are given out.

On March 7, we were hiding behind stage as we waited for Samantha to be knighted for exemplifying the quality of perseverance. Up until that day, we knew virtually nothing about this program. We'd heard Samantha talk about it a few times, but she's fairly tight-lipped about what goes on at school. Given the distractions so far that school year, we hadn't pressed her for more details on what the knighting ceremonies were all about. As we stood behind the curtain, we quietly made our way to the front of the procession of parents when we knew it was her turn. We listened to the school nurse, whom we'd gotten to know very well in the months since the initial diagnosis, read a letter about why Sam was chosen. Through her words, we learned that since Sam's teacher was out on maternity leave, the decision on whom to select had actually been left to the kids in the class, and they'd voted using secret ballots, so the winner's name remained a mystery. As they announced her name, the cafeteria burst into applause; her friends jumped up to hug her, and she stepped toward the stage. The moment she saw me, she sprinted over; I dropped down to one knee and lifted her into my arms for a hug that felt like it lasted days, not mere seconds. We'd broken protocol a bit; she was supposed to get her medal first and hug her parents second, but my elation over her achievement blew through any sense of decorum.

She sat smiling at us from the gallery as the ceremony pressed onward, stood to take a picture with all of the winners when the final name had been called, and then took photographs with the knights, Beth, and me. As we walked back to her classroom holding hands, Sam was beaming; Beth was still trying not to cry, and I pretended my allergies caused my eyes to appear a bit dewy. When we rounded the corner to go down the final hallway leading up to her room, a sliver of a girl's head was peering out from the doorway. The moment Sam stepped into view, the girl leapt into the hallway and screamed to the rest of the class, "Our warrior is on her way!"

Our warrior. She wasn't the sick kid; she wasn't the one they had to handle gently or the one to choose last when it came time to play games. They didn't mock her illness or harass her on days when she clearly didn't feel like being at school; they chose her as their beacon of strength. Chemo hadn't slowed her down, and steroids hadn't dimmed her light; she was the one the other kids elected because she had endured hardship, and she'd never stopped fighting. Looking back, during the months of her chemo, she'd missed only one day of school following a treatment. Make no mistake, she felt the effects of the cocktail she was on. She was tired, groggy, and nauseated more days than not, but she never got so much as a cold. Even on her worst days, she would still get up from her nap, want to go bike riding, jump on the trampoline, or wrestle with her brother and me. And if she disagreed with what someone was doing and felt that an invisible line had been crossed, she was always ready to fight.

I look back and wonder how I could have been so foolish. I knew her, everything about her, yet some part of me had been convinced that she'd stop fighting because of her disease. In retrospect, I have to side with Dostoevsky's conjecture in *The Brothers Karamazov* where he says that the genesis of every fear I have is a lie that I've chosen to believe. I bought into the lie that an illness was stronger than the will God had given my daughter. I believed the falsehood that the treatment she was enduring would somehow crush her spirit. It was the sound of a seven-year-old girl uttering two words that shattered the lies and added to the healing of my weary heart; our warrior.

# Chapter Fourteen

# Tough Mudder

I GOT ELECTROCUTED THREE times this morning. I wasn't repairing an outlet at the house, playing with extension cords in the rain, or recreating that scene from *Lethal Weapon* with the jumper cables and wet sponges. I voluntarily subjected myself to this form of physical torture, and I paid for it. The shocks came from obstacles along a gauntlet of insanity known as the Tough Mudder. In the world of athletic challenges, I've done triathlons, half marathons, long-distance biking, and adventure races over the last couple of decades. Recently, I've enjoyed extreme obstacle courses because of the unorthodox training they require, the need to adapt to whatever may life before me, and the spirit of camaraderie they breed among participants on race day. I've now done a handful of Tough Mudders spanning ten to twelve miles with twenty-five to thirty military-style obstacles designed to at least bend (if not break) you physically, mentally, and emotionally. Over the course of the last few races, I've seen the manliest of men reduced to tears from claustrophobia, hypothermia, and electrocution. Sounds fun, right?

Let me take a moment for you to join me on a mental journey through my least favorite obstacle thus far. It was late January, with temperatures in the lower forties, winds around twenty miles per hour, and ten miles and twenty-five obstacles already behind me on the track. As a pair of friends and I approached one of the last challenges, it seemed easy enough from afar; you had to crawl about thirty feet under a wooden frame set a foot and a half above the ground. As we drew closer, other details came into view that quickly shifted my thinking in terms of the difficulty and discomfort I could expect. The first thing that added to the mix was that the ground beneath the boards had been churned into mud, meaning it would be slow going. The second item of note was the vast expanse of ice that had been spread over the mud, meaning it would be slow going on a slick, unstable, frigid surface. The final kicker was the worst of all: tiny yellow wires hanging down every twelve to eighteen inches, which were sure to deliver at least a little bit of a shock given they were wired into a car battery on the side of the obstacle.

Ever the risk taker, I was the first in my party of three to dive in. I started crawling through the obstacle on my stomach, my forearms and chest colliding with the ice, and I slipped under the first couple strands of wires without incident. It was on the third or fourth set that I was met with a painful, audible crack when a wire landed directly on my lower spine. As the surge of electricity pulsed through my body, I realized that backing out wasn't an option, and sitting still would accomplish nothing, so the only path was to plow through as hard and as fast as possible. I was hit by at least half a dozen wires along the way and then shocked two more times when I reached in from the end of the obstacle to pull out a fellow racer who had effectively become paralyzed when his muscles locked up from the combination of ice and electrocution. Did I mention that I paid to do this? Oddly enough, instead of wallowing in the midst of my misery or focusing on the pain I'd experienced, I found myself adrenalized, excited, and racing forward to tackle whatever obstacle was next. Perhaps a portion of the proceeds from this book should go to getting me some couch time with a shrink; I clearly have issues!

Training for an event like that obviously takes some preparation unless you want to bypass a lot of obstacles, spend an entire day completing the race, and endure a very painful recovery afterward. As part of my prerace regimen, I put in a lot of hours running, lifting weights, and coming up with a slew of peculiar exercises to mirror what I'll find on the course. One particularly effective training night was spent with alternating three-mile runs and ten to fifteen minutes on an elementary school playground swinging on monkey bars, hurdling park benches, and balancing on bike racks. With another race a few months ahead of me, I've already started to refine my training and set my eyes on the goal ahead.

In the midst of this preparation, I recognized a stark contrast in my approach to training physically versus spiritually. Why is it that I seek out the most significant physical challenges the world around me has to offer yet avoid any semblance of spiritual hardship as if it were the plague? Why will I devote hours to training my body for every obstacle I can imagine but spend no more than minutes a day (if that) reading my Bible or actively connecting with God? While I recognize that some of my deeper issues are uniquely mine, I think this one trips up a number of the Christians I know. I'm surrounded by friends and acquaintances that routinely participate in long-distance, competitive races. I would venture to guess that we share in the struggle to focus less on improving our physical abilities and devote more of our lives to maturing spiritually.

With that in mind, I wondered how different my world might look if I sought out spiritual challenges, deepened my biblical knowledge, and viewed hardships as something to overcome instead of obstacles to avoid. While I know the situation itself wouldn't be any different, I believe that my perspective would entirely change. The Bible calls upon us to look for God in all circumstances, but I repeatedly find myself avoiding Him when troubles arise. Through some confluence of pride, a need for control, and a desire to disassociate God with the darker facets of life, I relegate Him to more proper places for His presence: church, service projects, or prayer time. Yet if I simply flip open the Bible, I find that scripture calls for the opposite, particularly in times of intense suffering.

Few books in the Bible bring forth a more immediate mental picture of physical and emotional suffering than Job. When wrestling with the trials he's facing, Job listens to the opinions of several of his friends; one of whom speaks of stepping past the temporal pain of the moment to embrace the presence of God in all things. In verses 8 and 9 of chapter 5, this friend challenges Job to wrap up his pity party and says, "But if I were you, I would appeal to God; I would lay my cause before Him. He performs wonders that cannot be fathomed, miracles that cannot be counted."

As I navigate the emotional and spiritual trials before me during my daughter's illness, will I strive to view them as challenges to overcome or conflicts to avoid? When God calls me to move in a way that causes discomfort, will I pretend it's just another obstacle in a race I've paid to run and hit it with everything I've got? I'm not brave enough to tell Him to do His worst quite yet, but once you've been chilled and electrocuted at the same time, you start to think you can handle whatever lies before you. With eyes fully focused on Him, I'm starting to think there's a chance that's true.

# Chapter Fifteen

# Sermon

Date: Thursday, 15 March 2012
Hey guys! Hope you are having a great spring break!

I wanted to let you all know that Chris is talking this Sunday at the Vine (11:00). Please come! He just practiced his talk on me, and I was bawling the whole time (and laughing too). We both know that God wants us to share what has been going on with our family this year, so when Matt and Aaron asked him to do a lesson on joy, he initially said no (out of fear) . . . then called Matt back and said yes. He is talking about my daughter and her autoimmune disease. He is really nervous. Talking in Sunday school and talking in front of a hundred people is completely different. Please pray for people's hearts to be touched.

Thanks guys! He doesn't know I am sending you guys this email. He would be embarrassed if I told you all to come listen to him talk. He's really a pretty modest guy. Please pray for his strength to do this. He will be crying, I can promise you that! Public crying is hard for men!

Luv ya,
Beth

I'LL GO AHEAD and put this out there: the reason most of us don't give our numbers to pastors is to avoid the message I got a few days ago. It was the music director for the contemporary service, who is something of a hipster, so thankfully he communicated via text. He let me know that the church was doing a sermon on joy that Sunday and that they wanted a few short clips of church members talking about the ways that joy was present in their lives. I sat, staring at the phone for a few moments, trying to suppress my instinctive reaction of, "not a chance." I crafted a politically correct text to convey that joy honestly hadn't been a huge part of my world over the last year or so. Could I talk about being prayerful? Absolutely. Could I speak about the concept of acceptance? Maybe. But the word *joy* didn't come to mind very often during that era. He wrote back that he understood and even apologized for asking, saying he just thought it would be very meaningful if our family had something to share in light of all we'd endured.

There was also an ulterior motive in my reply; I detest the idea of public speaking. My wife will be quick to tell you it has nothing to do with confidence; I have more than enough of that. It's also not that I'm wildly socially awkward; I tend to connect with people and convey my thoughts pretty well in everyday conversation. I suppose my natural introversion is to blame, making talking in front of a large group of people the last thing I'd ever want to do. When I found a way to decline the offer to speak, the part of me that initially recoiled at the idea was put at ease.

I closed my eyes for a moment and started to pray, assuring God I'd follow through on some future opportunity to answer that call when it was at the right time and the right topic. That's when God showed me a whirlwind of mental images, revealing the places where joy had been my companion in recent times. It was as if someone created a collage of letters, meals, gifts, hugs, phone calls, smiles, and prayers from that period and condensed all of them into a thirty-second strip of film.

It was fifteen minutes later that I found myself holding my phone, reversing my attitude from the initial text, and saying I'd be honored to add to the service if they hadn't already filled my slot. I knew it meant stepping outside of my comfort zone, but I suppose that's what it means to be faithful, right?

In the days that followed, God gave me ample opportunity to show that faithfulness. What started as a two-to-three-minute video clip turned into five to eight minutes, with a request that I speak in person, if I were willing. The idea of standing at a pulpit was unsettling, but I pretended that I was just writing out a script and refused to focus on the part where I'd have to actually say it in public. With a pen and notepad in hand, I sat and prayed for God to guide my articulation of His joyous presence in my life. I started jotting down whatever came to mind and quickly found myself flipping the page because I'd run out of space on the first sheet. After filling several pages with ideas, I tried to organize and condense them, creating what the business world would call an executive summary. When I stopped writing and read my summary out loud, I had a bit of a problem; it was taking over ten minutes to say everything. I decided I'd go back through and cull superfluous commentary, but in the end, I succeeded in adding material, not taking it out. It was already the Thursday before the Sunday service, so the time to arrange it all was dwindling rapidly. Realizing I was in over my head, I sat down with the pastor, Matt Stone, and the music director, Aaron Hale, to get advice on what I should remove from my talk. When I went to speak with them, I didn't have a notepad, cheat sheet, or even an outline, I just started saying all the things God had shown me over the previous few days. I told them about hard times, happy times, and all of the places in between. I know that my words weren't the most eloquent, but I wasn't pulling any punches and exposed some of the raw, painful realities and questions that a father asks when one of his children is suffering. By the time I finished talking, Matt checked his watch and told me that I'd been speaking for over twenty minutes. He's a man of few words, but I could see the wheels turning in his mind when he said "I'd have to say that's a heck of a sermon, Mr. Slaughter." He looked over at Aaron; the two of them nodded at each other, and Matt asked me if I could do the exact same thing when Sunday morning rolled around. Some subconscious part of me said yes while the rest of me recovered from the experience of expressing so many intimate things out loud. I hardly noticed when they set to the task of rearranging the church service to take out Matt's intended sermon and effectively give me free reign to say whatever words God put in my mouth.

I hope nothing here is coming across with a tinge of arrogance; the days from that first text to the morning I spoke had nothing to do with my ability and everything to do with God showing me what could be done if I followed His lead. I so often operate in my sphere of relative comfort that it clouds my vision of God's involvement because I have the opportunity to congratulate myself on all I've accomplished. I struggle to remember that no matter how bright the moon in the night sky may be, it produces no light of its own; it merely reflects a greater source of illumination. By moving into a place where I knew I was wildly incapable, I was free to observe God in action. I was able to witness the way He can take something broken, insufficient, and worldly and turn it into something incredible, powerful, and divine. Instead of growing more nervous as Sunday approached, I found myself at peace with the idea of playing pastor for a morning.

There were plenty of distractions afoot leading up to the sermon, including my wife coming down with pneumonia. Of course, when you have a severe cold and decide to run five miles two days in a row, that sort of thing can happen—twice—in just over a year. Beth, I love you, but you're a spaz. So when Sunday morning rolled around, it ended up being just me at church, with Beth and the kids staying at home to recover. In truth, that was a bit of a blessing in disguise. It wasn't that I would be more nervous about speaking with them there, but the wounds were still so fresh when it came to Samantha's illness that I worried it would derail my train of thought if I looked out and saw my family's faces. I also knew I'd be expressing some moments of doubt, frustration, anger, and rebellion, and I wasn't quite sure that I was ready for my kids to hear those messages.

Much to my personal chagrin, there weren't a lot of open chairs that morning; so as I waited to take the stage, my nervousness started to build. I kept telling myself that I didn't have to be nervous because I wasn't relying on me for anything that was about to happen, which helped a little. I had a single index card with no more than two dozen words scratched out in pencil to serve as a rough outline for the sermon, but I intentionally kept it from being scripted to give God room to work through me. As I sat on a stool in front of a huge group of people, I said one final prayer before opening my mouth and spilling my heart to the friends gathered there with me.

I honestly can't recall what I said that morning. I remember seeing faces filled with laughter, eyes filled with tears, and more sympathetic half smiles than I could possibly count. Matt gave me a video of the service, but I've yet to watch it. I know God was present there because I've had multiple people walk up to me and greet me by name, telling me they were there that morning and were touched by how candid I was in talking about finding joy in the midst of suffering. I realize now that we have a tendency to hide our heartache instead of wear it on our sleeves, leaving those enduring hardships in the lurch when it comes to connecting. We are a broken people, living in a broken world, yet we always want to appear as if we have it all figured out. I think there's something to be said for exposing that brokenness to show how God has moved in our lives and to give those who don't have it all figured out an opportunity to belong to a community of believers who are working through difficult times too. When a person in the midst of a struggle is questioning God's divinity, power, and love, it's nearly impossible to find commiseration in the midst of a church full of perfect people.

I know from Romans 3:10 that "there is no one righteous, not even one," so why do I try so hard to appear as if I am? I know that I should strive to be righteous, but that's very different from expending an inordinate amount of energy to convince everyone that I have it all under control when I don't. By accepting my own inadequacies, not only would I free up more of my energy to serve God, but I would also make myself a more approachable Christian to the world around me that desperately wants to find a place to belong when hardships arise.

I am continually amazed by how God takes the moments we think will be most terrifying, painful, and unsuccessful and uses them to display His glory. I hope to be less satisfied with my comfort zone in the years to come and find the courage to tread more narrow paths, knowing His power will remain steadfast when my strength fails.

# Chapter Sixteen

# Weariness

I'M BEYOND SICK of nights like this. Thankfully, Sam's last infusions were half a year ago, and we've been able to avoid going back into Texas Children's for months because she's doing so well.

For quite a while, she was tolerant of me giving her injections of chemo at home. I admittedly wasn't the best shot giver in the world at the onset. I worried about jabbing the needle in too far, at the wrong angle, or in a way that didn't leave space to push the full dosage into her stomach in a single shot. Over time, though, I was less often to nick a blood vessel, grew faster with the injections, and was able to get her through the weekly ordeal with less discomfort and reluctance. I also procured the topical cold spray they used in the infusion center to numb the flesh of her stomach, which helped things flow far more smoothly.

As the weeks turned to months, however, her cooperation waned. I'm not sure if she just grew tired of the shots, if a new batch of methotrexate made it more uncomfortable, or if it was more painful for other reasons; but coercing her to acquiesce to injections became increasingly difficult. Initially, the allure of pulling something out of the prize box we keep in our closet made it only a minor fight. But eventually, it became more of a raging battle the moment she realized it was time for her shot. There were moments of verbal rebellion, where she would scream and yell at me, telling me I was hurting her and that she wanted me to stop. At other times, she would resort to stealth, hiding herself away somewhere in the house as I walked around with an alcohol wipe in one hand, cold spray in the other, and a syringe full of chemo held between my teeth. Then there were the real fights—kicking, punching, screaming, and then some. When that kid flips the switch and decides to go primal, she's nearly impossible to control in a way that doesn't do her harm. But to hold her down and try to keep her still enough to pump a syringe full of chemo in without hitting a blood vessel or having the needle go into muscle is virtually impossible. I tried to reason with her, told her the injections were the worst part of my week too but that I had to cause her some momentary pain to ensure she experienced complete healing in the long run. Some days, that would calm her down for a moment, just long enough; but over the last month or two, I've had to drag her down to the ground, force her onto her back, pin her body using my legs, and prepare to time the injections between fits of violent struggle to cause as little damage as possible.

Just before I inject her, her voice rings out, "I'll do it, just stop holding me down!" Even in the midst of pain and fear, she still chooses to allow me to do it rather than force me to go on against her will. She takes the higher path in healing, the one where she is still willing to be healed, even when it hurts. That momentary reprieve in her attitude helps more than she knows. I'm yet to truly inject her without her consent, and I pray that I never have to. I worry carrying that out against her will may somehow change how she sees me. I'm already the calloused, emotionless guy hurting her once a week, but to have her see me as so devoid of compassion that I could do it even while she's truly trying to stop me may break something about her vision of me as a father. Please, God, take this cup from me . . .

The moment the injection is finished, I release her, and she runs up to her room, slams the door, and sits on her bed, crying as the feeling of sickness overtakes her. I do much the same though slamming the door doesn't seem necessary, so I avoid that part of the reaction. The punching bag beckons me, but I've learned to mute its call. As soon as my composure returns, I make my way upstairs and into her room, where I sit on the bed next to her and scoop her into my arms. She doesn't push me away; she knows that I'm hurting her to help her, but the pain of the moment blinds her to that when the healing elixir is administered. We sit there entwined as one—her tears visible, mine tucked away, until the suffering subsides.

I've come to realize that she's much more of a man than I. She takes on the pain that comes from healing the deficiency deep within her and always chooses to allow it when the moment of truth arrives. I can't say that I do the same. Even with my tendency to tolerate or tune out pain, I tend to exercise that during periods of indulgence, not periods of improvement. I would generally rather avoid the discomfort that arises from addressing deeper-rooted issues, and when the opportunity to heal through what I deem to be too painful a medium arises, I fight every step of the way. That never changes the events ordained to pass; it only shows my weakness when going through them. I also tend to view the type of deity that would either cause or allow suffering as one lacking understanding, or not possessing omniscience, because if He truly cared, He'd find an easier way (easier for me, that is) to get His point across.

I'm going to work on that innate response from now on. Being on the side of the healer, knowing that what I'm doing is needed to bring restoration to my daughter shifts my point of view. When I'm looking in the mirror with tears in my eyes, I picture God feeling the same way about whatever healing He's trying to accomplish in me. He doesn't do that, I know, because He's at least a little bit smarter than I am. I see this moment in time, this temporary suffering, and can't fully appreciate the healing it will provide. For one that sits beyond the spectrum of time, He doesn't see the pain of healing; He sees the radiance of the healed. What's to be already is, so even as I struggle with today's suffering and look to the uncertainty of the future, He smiles at the victory already achieved. Every once in a while, late at night after her injection, I pretend I see the world that way too. Yet I know full well that a week later, I'll be right back where I began—pained in the moment and struggling to be hopeful for the future.

# Chapter Seventeen

# The F-word

Date: Wednesday, 9 January 2013

Thank you so much for the prayers! We had our third doctor's appt today at TX Children's, and they told us that she has severe vertigo. They did tons of tests today. She was so worn out that she came home and slept for four hours straight! They predict that she will not be better for about a month! She is so dizzy that she is having trouble sitting up straight and can't walk without holding my hand. She can't even go to school because she is seeing double—for a month! Yikes! But the awesome news is that we went to her second appt today, and her doctor said she can finally stop taking the chemo shots . . . forever! She is sooo dang excited! And so are Chris and I!

I have a sitter coming over all day tomorrow! I will see you guys in class! I have got to get out of this house!

Prayer is amazing! Thanks girls!

Beth

JANUARY 9, 2013. We'd been anxiously awaiting that date for three months. At Samantha's quarterly checkup with the rheumatology group in October 2012, they'd been so impressed and dumbfounded by her healing that the two- or three-year-cycle of chemo she was on could be cut short if she had no active lesions or signs of worsening by her January appointment. There are milestones in a child's life that are worth celebrating: first words, first steps, first days of school. So it was with some irony that at only eight years of age, the milestone on which we were most focused was being done, not starting anew. There were talks of parties, celebrations, and even a quick vacation to collectively shout a cry of relief that her long-fought battle was finally over. We were going to be *finished* (that's the f-word I was talking about); shame on you if you thought it was something else—sinner.

But as that date drew nearer, and the finish line was less of a mirage in the distance and more of a banner just out of reach, a new obstacle presented itself. In her eighteen months on various doses of chemo, Samantha had never been sick. Not a single time. My wife's obsession with keeping Sam healthy by bathing her in Purell and force-feeding her lemons from the trees in our backyard had paid off. Then, just a day or two before Christmas in 2012, a cold that started with Beth spread to Sam. Things seemed run-of-the-mill—congestion, runny nose, sore throat, mild fever. The normal life cycle of the virus drew near, but instead of improving entirely, Samantha started to have trouble balancing when she made her way through the house at typical breakneck speed. Over the course of a couple of days, her condition grew worse, and she complained of constant spinning and dizziness, growing more pronounced every time she closed her eyes or went horizontal. During her cold, she'd complained of pain in her right ear, so we thought she'd developed some kind of ear infection that was causing problems with her balance. The PA at our local RediClinic (all the doctor's offices were closed for the holidays) hypothesized that we were probably right although no active infection was visible. Nonetheless, a cycle of antibiotics ensued, and there was a hope that when New Year's rolled around, all would be well, and we could refocus our sights on January 9.

As the days passed, Samantha's condition didn't improve. She remained unsteady when walking and resorted to keeping a hand against a wall, bookcase, or couch to help her balance. I took her in to see her general pediatrician, who concurred that she was likely still experiencing congestion or pressure from her cold or a subsequent infection and that the best approach was to wait and see if she improved on her own. By this point, the vertigo had grown so severe that the only way to get her to sleep was to give her Phenergan (for those not familiar, that's not a pill you swallow; it has a different point of entry that's quite unpleasant). Under the influence of that drug, the room stopped spinning long enough for her to fall asleep. During the day, it was a well-timed combination of Dramamine, Bonine, and Zofran to cope with the symptoms. Generally speaking, she was making small improvements in her mobility without assistance and learning to cope by playing games that allowed her to sit so the dizziness wasn't as pronounced. But when her condition hadn't dramatically improved by the first week of January, an appointment with a pediatric ENT was made for the same day as the rheumatology appointment we'd been looking forward to for so long. A day that was intended to be pure exaltation had become another source of concern, another unknown outcome to fear, and another reset of the finish line we thought we were about to cross.

After a hearing test and examination by the ENT, she was diagnosed with severe vertigo that was either the result of inflammation in the labyrinth behind the ear that controls balance or potentially some degree of damage to her vestibular nerve resulting from the cold she'd had a couple of weeks before. In either case, there was no cause for immediate concern about something more dangerous, but there was no remedy in sight either. Both conditions had no real cure and carried recovery times of at least weeks, potentially months.

I write this chapter on January 11, her struggle with balance still ongoing. I find myself disappointed in my own inability to dial back the fear for her new ailment long enough to truly celebrate the beauty of what she has already overcome. The presence of a new battle shouldn't negate the victory over an enemy already defeated. Life is like that, isn't it? Just as the majestic and numinous manifests itself in blinding splendor and warms our hearts, an eruption of darkness overshadows the brilliance of the praiseworthy and throws a cold blanket over our souls. Why do we allow that? Why do we turn away from the glory of what God has done and instead focus on what He's failing to do? I know the outcome of her current ailment is in no way changed by my fear.

Yet the silver-tongued voice of the enemy tickles my ear time and time again. *God gave her one miraculous healing; you're a fool to expect another. She won't be as lucky this time as she was before. If you aren't afraid for her, it means you don't love her. And if He truly loved her, why would He allow her to suffer like this again? Some healer . . .*

Once more, I'm drawn out of the darkness, not by my own faith and strength but by the sound of those who refuse to succumb. As I was washing dishes downstairs and giving Beth an escape from the house in which she's been confined of late, I heard an earth-shattering *kaboom* from upstairs. Assuming Sam lost her balance and was hurt, I rushed to the stairs, only to be met by the sound of laughter coming from both kids.

Despite Samantha's dizziness, she refused to just sit around and mope. She still insisted on trying to do everything on her own and would very reluctantly ask for help only in the most extreme circumstances. There were times where her vision was distorted, creating a double view of everything in front of her. Apparently, while she was attempting to play chase with Noah, she approached the doorway leading into Noah's room, only to find two doors in front of her. Still moving full throttle, she took a gamble and opted for the door on the right, which turned out to be the wrong choice. As I crested the staircase, I found the two of them lying on the floor, rolling with laughter so violently that they had trouble explaining what had happened. Sam had a red stripe where her forehead and cheek had collided with the wall, but instead of complaining or crying in pain and frustration, she just said, "Well, I guess I should pick the left one next time." She then popped up and started running in an erratic fashion to get the game back on track. When the going gets tough, kids don't lie down and wallow in self-pity; they find a way to rise up and keep on being kids.

As Christians, it is our calling to do the same. As Psalm 55:22 reminds us, we are to cast aside our fears and the snares that tempt us to become something we are not; we are to step past the distractions of circumstance and remain steadfast in our faith. We are going to face hard times, we are going to suffer, we are going to be weary, but joy awaits those who move through those periods, not those who anchor themselves to the afflictions that plague us.

Instead of returning to the Psalm, as I often do, I hear words spoken in the New Testament that couldn't be more fitting. Jesus says in Matthew 18:3, "Truly, I tell you, unless you change and become like little children, you will never enter the kingdom of heaven." When I don't know which way to go, I'm reminded to take a risk and keep moving anyway. When my gamble doesn't pay off, I'm called to laugh, pick myself up, and get back to running the race that lies before me with the jubilant heart of a child.

# Chapter Eighteen

# Under the Influence

1) Plaquenil (pill)
2) Folic Acid (pill)
3) Keflex (pill)
4) Methatrexate (shot/IV)
5) Phenergan (yucky)
6) Solumedrol (IV)
7) Dovonex (lotion)
8) Clobetasol Propionate (lotion)
9) Ibuprofen (pill)
10) Acetamenophin (pill)
11) Dramamine (pill)
12) Bonine (pill)
13) Benadryl (pill)
14) Lidocaine (lotion)
15) Atropine (IV)

FOR A MATH assignment, Sam had to learn how to make a bar chart. After she tired of the concepts of counting Skittles, birds, and other commonplace things, she got the idea that we should list out the medications she'd taken over the last year and make a bar chart out of how she had to take them. For those of you familiar with Phenergan, you'll understand why she wasn't a fan of including that method of administration in the graph.

I have come to the realization, over the last few weeks, that humans possess an uncanny ability to mask weakness. I remember the professor of my psychology class in college talking about a patient with a split-brain. For extreme seizures, the final line of treatment involves severing some of the ties between the left and right halves of the brain, rendering the normal communication path between the two sides useless. After that operation, it's possible to communicate information to one side of the brain (one ear, but not the other, for example) without communicating it to both sides. So in a somewhat sadistic study, they practiced just that, not only to gauge how a patient would behave, but to see how he would explain his behaviors if he didn't know where the instructions to act had come from. With headphones on, but the volume only dialed up on one ear, the scientists would give a command, and the man would begin to carry out the task he was beckoned to do. When asked why he was doing it, his brain was so adept at maintaining the illusion of control that it would concoct an artificial reason to explain the behavior. The scientist would whisper, "Stand up, go to the door, and start to go down the hall." Once the man crossed the threshold of the door, someone would ask where he was going, and he would explain that he decided it would behoove him to go back to his room to grab an umbrella since he heard it might rain later that day. I found that ability to mask incredibly intriguing, and I've now had a chance to witness it firsthand.

When Samantha started to complain about her dizziness, it didn't seem to be too severe. She only mentioned it every once in a while, and when asked, she would say she felt fine, but then I really started to watch her. I noticed that she was moving in a strategic fashion. She was walking along walls or cabinets, barely brushing against them to maintain her balance but with such subtlety that it wasn't obvious. She would also pretend to walk in odd ways, pirouetting on her toes or skipping, to hide how difficult it was to walk without falling over. In the same way, when the spinning got really intense, she would make eye contact with me for a moment but then look past or around me, as if searching for something just beyond where I was standing. It was only upon direct questioning that she admitted that it was getting hard to focus on me without seeing two of me. At the visit with the ENT, he had her stand up so he could gauge her level of instability. I watched with a small grin as she slid down from the exam table and sneakily stood with her heels barely touching the footrest of the table, giving her extra balance. The doctor's face momentarily registered surprise before he looked down and saw what she was doing. After having her move forward a few inches, she instantly toppled once the trickery was removed from the equation.

We live in a culture that thrives on the ability to mask and concoct elaborate parapets of success, happiness, and everything-is-all-right attitudes to keep people from seeing how unstable we truly are. The knee-jerk response to questions about our well-being is that we're fine, which may or may not have anything to do with the reality of our condition. While we'd like to attribute that behavior to something as noble as not inconveniencing others, the more frequent cause is an unwillingness to embrace our own inabilities. If we mention that we're not fine or ask for help, it's confessing that we can't handle it alone, and nothing about our social structure suggests that to be an acceptable attitude. But then there's Jesus. He calls us to admit our inadequacies. He beckons us along a path with Him that demands we abandon our cultural mind-set and embrace that we alone are insufficient. We are told that no matter how grandiose our works, the path to salvation is reserved for those who die to themselves so they can be reborn of His love.

A final thought on the events of the last two weeks: we are a medicated people. When Sam's affliction with dizziness began, the first thing we did was pump her full of a myriad of drugs to subdue the effects of her ailment. If we gave her enough of what was at our disposal, we could get her back to normal—which is what any loving parent would do, right? So imagine my surprise during the visit with the ENT when he suggested exactly the opposite. Of the two potential diagnoses for Samantha, the more extreme one involved a virus that had inflamed or damaged her vestibular nerve, which affects both balance and hearing. To the extent some damage had occurred, he said, the body possessed a remarkable ability to heal itself in time. If that nerve had unlearned what it meant to be balanced, with enough exposure to being off kilter, it would simply relearn what balance was. The medicines Sam was being fed throughout the day (and night) limited her body's ability to experience the full effect of her dizziness, and we were actually retarding the healing process.

How often, in the midst of difficult times, do we attempt to simply bypass the hard part with some form of distraction? If we want to mature and grow in strength as believers, every once in a while, we need to set the distractions aside and hit our fears head-on. If we turn to scripture, we find countless stories of outnumbered armies, impossible odds, and unlikely heroes who overcame the obstacles before them when they called upon God to strengthen them. They weren't immune to hardships; they were confronted by them on a constant basis. But they placed their trust in God, knowing that when their strength faltered, His would be sufficient. When we lean on our own methods of coping, we deprive ourselves the opportunity to place our trust in Him. Doing so not only avoids the problem, but it becomes a missed chance to strengthen our faith. We need to blow back the fog in which we clothe ourselves and allow Him to lift us above the challenges that lie in our path. It is only when we confront our demons that we can finally look up and see those obstacles in the rearview mirror once and for all.

## Chapter Nineteen

# Begin Again

O N THE MORNING of January 12, the kids and I embarked on a Saturday morning journey that had become a routine for us over time. When Noah was still a baby and often woke at five in the morning, my wife was already exhausted by the time dawn crept over the horizon. Instead of truly being a great husband and waking up at that hour, I tried to be a decent husband and got the kids out of the house around seven thirty or eight so that she could climb back in bed to get a little extra rest. We would generally go grab breakfast somewhere but nowhere quite as much as Taco Cabana. Aside from the preference to go to a place that isn't loaded down with other children climbing all over playgrounds and exposing one another to who knows what kind of germs, the quantity of food that my two kids eat there is mind-boggling. It's like they put crack in the tortillas; they usually each eat three breakfast tacos loaded with eggs, potatoes, and bacon. So on the twelfth, the three of us drove over, ordered our mini-buffet, and sat at a table, waiting for our food to arrive.

Another thing we always do on those mornings is play games together. We might bring cards, books, or board games; but on that morning, we were just making up games of our own. A favorite of ours is to start with the letter *A* and name an animal, then have the next person name one starting with *B*, and so on, until we've covered the entire alphabet. Normally, once Sam knows which letter she is starting with, she mentally runs through all of the ones she'll have to do and come up with funny names for some of them while Noah and I are still fumbling around with the first few letters of the alphabet. On that particular Saturday, she started with alligator for *A*, I said buffalo for *B*, and Noah said cheetah for *C*. After Noah's turn, we looked over to hear her choice for *D*, but she made a confused face and then frowned. I asked if she couldn't think of an animal, and she replied with "What comes after the letter *C*?" At first, I thought she was joking, but it quickly became evident that she truly didn't know the next letter in the alphabet. I kept asking questions and trying to hide my panic, but it didn't take long to realize that she couldn't remember the days of the week, months of the year, or people's birthdays. I gathered our food, tossed it in a bag, and climbed into the car as I called Beth to let her know that I'd be dropping Noah off at home and taking Samantha straight to Texas Children's. It was painfully obvious that we were no longer just dealing with an inner-ear issue.

The hours that followed were a whirlwind. Once Sam and I arrived at the ER, we were quickly ushered into a room where the attending physician examined her. You can always tell when a doctor has checked her file because they walk in with a blend of intrigue and terror on their faces. Given the wide eyes and downward glance at Sam's leg, I knew that this doctor had clearly seen her medical record just before coming in. She began by asking me to explain everything that happened that morning, attempting to process the odd combination of symptoms I was describing. Sam seemed to be losing mental capacity by the minute and, at that point, was unable to distinguish colors (it all looked white or gray) or sit up straight, and she had trouble talking from time to time. My first thought was either some kind of stroke or a tumor pressing on the part of her brain that handled memory and sensory information. The doctor was moving down the same line of thinking, but some of the problems Sam was having didn't seem to fit with that opinion. Nonetheless, since those were the most likely candidates, we would need to do an MRI of her brain to rule out a stroke or tumor. The problem with doing an MRI of her brain was that it required sedation (no chance of toughing it out like her first MRI), and since she'd just eaten breakfast, we'd have to wait several hours to be sure there was no chance of her aspirating when she was put under.

I called Beth to let her know we had to wait before they could do the MRI. She was busily phoning friends to find a place for Noah to spend the night so she could join us in the ER. I knew she was upset and afraid for Sam, but there was something else in her voice that made me ask what was wrong. Noah—who could sense that Sam's new symptoms were far more disconcerting than her linear morphea—had just asked, "Mom, is Samantha going to die?" The agony in Beth's voice wasn't because of the question, but because she truly didn't know the answer.

# Chapter Twenty

# My Way

SAMANTHA'S LUCIDITY EBBED and flowed from one moment to the next, but her symptoms continued to worsen as the day progressed. At nearly eight at night, they were finally ready to do the MRI of her brain. She was wheeled into the prep room with the anesthesiologist, who went to work checking her file and measuring out a dosage of sedatives to put her to sleep. Since my daughter is me through and through, I knew that she might have an adverse reaction to the medication, but the intensity of her response surprised even me. The first syringe of drugs pushed her into a sleeplike trance, but it was like a cold blanket that she rose to throw off after a few seconds. I grabbed her as she reached up to claw at her IV, and the anesthesiologist quickly pumped in a second syringe of milky chemicals, which dropped her onto the bed a moment later. We watched as she was rolled into the MRI room, fully under the influence of the drugs. Until, that is, a nurse leaned over to adjust Sam's blanket and found herself flailing backward when Sam picked a leg up and landed a heel dead center in the nurse's chest. A third, and presumably final, dose of sedatives was given, and she drifted off to sleep.

The MRI itself had to be done first without and then with contrast to evaluate blood flow in her brain and confirm whether or not a tumor or stroke was the cause of her problems. It was an hour-long procedure, and the clock seemed to be at a standstill as we waited for her to emerge. On the plus side, while she was sedated, the team in the ER was going to go in and handle a spinal tap to see if there was any swelling, inflammation, or evidence of infection in her brain. It seemed like a short eternity before a nurse emerged to let us know that Sam was in the recovery room and ready for us to join her.

In the aftermath of the MRI, Sam slowly began to wake from the heavy dosage of drugs needed to subdue her. To say that she woke up bright eyed and bushy tailed would be a lie. She woke up pissed—really, really pissed. Once we made it out of the recovery area and back into the room in the ER where she'd already spent over eight hours that day, she pushed back the haze of sedation and let the intensity of her anger be known. Her reaction was so sudden, intense, and violent that it took only a moment to clear the room of everyone but her and me. At first, I was sitting on the foot of the bed with her while she screamed, thrashed, and started tearing at the sheets before hurling them across the room. I kept reminding her that the medicine she'd been given would make her uncomfortable, that her body would want to be active to flush the drugs out, and that it might be hard to control her emotions. She yelled that she wanted to leave and cried out that she was done being subjected to tests. All of that I allowed until she reached across to her arm, trying to rip out her IV. I gripped her wrist and pried it away, forcing her to loosen her hold on the tubing that was running into her vein. She fought me, swinging at my hand, clawing at my fingers, telling me to let her go and that she didn't want me to touch her. Without giving her time to react, I lifted her from the bed, slid in behind her, pulled her back against my chest, and wrapped my arms around the front of her body. From that angle, I could allow her to continue thrashing and fighting, but I could also control both of her arms if she tried to pull her IV out again, which she attempted multiple times. For nearly fifteen minutes, I held her like that, her back to my chest, my arms encircling her. She threw everything she could reach across the room; the screaming didn't stop for more than an instant, and she resorted to biting me to try to break my hold on her. At one point, she was flailing on the bed in a fit of rage, her heels slamming into the metal frame that surrounded her. Once she realized that wasn't getting a reaction, she started pounding her heels down into the mattress, then began using the heel of one leg to kick herself in the other shin. She was kicking hard enough to do damage, and I quietly whispered that she should stop, that she was only going to hurt herself. Her reply, with tear-filled eyes was simple, "I want to hurt myself." If you've read the pressure cooker chapter, that should sound regrettably familiar.

In that moment, my prayer for strength and wisdom was answered when God reminded me how often I'd been the kid doing the kicking, screaming, and trying to hurt myself just to get away from His loving embrace. All those moments in my life where I would convince myself

He wasn't there, when in fact, He was holding me against His chest, whispering words of love that my selfish cries entirely drowned out. I wanted things to be my way, not His. His way hurt too much; His way wasn't what I wanted; His way was just that—His. And in my rebellion, I would rather suffer than submit. I would walk away from the healer, blaming Him for the affliction all the while, never stopping to see that what I was enduring was ultimately going to render me better than I was before the pain began.

As the peace of that realization washed over me, the sensation must have been palpable. A few minutes later, her fists stopped flying, she stopped spitting, and she quit biting. She dropped her head onto my arms, and she cried as one defeated, perhaps even rescued, after a long battle. I eased my grip as a protector and embraced her as a father until her tears ran dry and the beast became a child once more. In typical Samantha fashion, her first words were "Truth or dare?" You always have to pick dare in our house. I answered with "Dare," to which she replied, "I dare you to go get the car and take me home." I laughed for the first time in a few hours, and she softly laughed with me, knowing my answer would be no but understanding that denying her what she wanted was best for her healing.

I often think about how I am supposed to approach God during painful times, and it's honestly not an area where I move with grace and genuflection. I found it both surprising and refreshing that He would choose a day spent in fear for Samantha's safety as a platform to give me a different perspective. I was afforded an opportunity to be like Him, to better understand how He feels when we rebel—to know how His heart breaks when we reject Him, scream at Him, try to run away from Him, and even hurt ourselves out of some sense of injustice from a circumstance for which we blame Him. In that hospital room, with my child pulled to my chest, I saw my relationship with Him through His eyes in a very real and raw fashion. Because of that, I was filled with a kind of love that I've so often lacked in the day-to-day routine of my life. Of course, I love my children; of course, I love my wife, but this kind of love was something different. It was a feeling akin to the first few chapters of Hosea, where God again and again brings a wayward sinner back to Him in spite of all of the mistakes and infidelities intentionally committed. Sitting in that hospital bed, my love for Sam was undeterred by rejection, unconcerned with acceptance, and exclusively focused on protecting my beloved, whether she wanted that love or not. Knowing all the while that, in time, she would understand that love to be true and would want nothing more than to be held by me until her cries ceased and a glimmer of happiness returned to her heart.

# Chapter Twenty-One

# Scarlet Letter

I T HAD BEEN a long day—twelve hours in the emergency room, an MRI, and a spinal tap before we were admitted for an overnight stay and in a room on the neurology floor of the hospital. As the nurse acclimated us to our new location, she reached into her pocket and pulled out a bright yellow band of plastic. After she affixed the bracelet to Samantha's wrist, I saw the dark bold letters spelling out, "FALL RISK." I didn't know why, but the sight of those words adorning her tiny, helpless hand caused a surge of rage deep within me.

It reminded me of the night I'd visited my father in the ICU at St. Luke's after his stroke, when the right side of his body remained unresponsive to his mind's instructions. In his case, in spite of some of his body's limitations, his obstinate nature remained fully functional, earning him the same bracelet Samantha was now wearing. While in ICU, he continually ignored the staff's pleadings to ask them for help, and he frequently came crashing to the floor. He wasn't willing to admit he had a problem and was even less likely to ask someone to help him get from one place to another. By the time he left the hospital a couple of weeks later, he was littered with cuts and bruises from his numerous attempts to get up and walk around just like he'd done before his stroke.

When it was his stubbornness earning him the bracelet, it somehow seemed fitting. Now that it was strapped on the wrist of my little girl who had done nothing to deserve it, it just didn't seem right. And yet it was. She couldn't walk on her own; in fact, she'd gotten to the point where she couldn't stand or sit up straight without falling over. My wife, Samantha, and I knew it, but none of us wanted it to be brought to light. It was like a scarlet letter we didn't want to force her to wear for the entire world to see.

We're like that when it comes to our weaknesses, or at least I am. I can recognize and be fully aware of my own deficiencies, but those are my crosses to bear, my problems to solve privately. I don't want or need anyone's assistance in remedying what afflicts me. This is a combination of my obstinate nature, pride, unwillingness to admit my inabilities, and a desire not to impose on others. I've been independent for as long as I can remember, so relying on someone else is as unnatural an act as I can imagine.

When I thought about my tendency to keep my weaknesses tucked away, I came to another realization. Our sin is like that too, or at least mine is. It's not meant for public consumption, not intended for anyone but the bearer to know. Religion isn't a team sport; I've always said that. Our problems are for us to work out with God or to not work out at all. But what if our wrists were plastered with our single greatest sin, our most profound weakness? There would, of course, be predators that would use that indication to lead others astray. They would prey upon those faults and use them to manipulate us into a situation that would leave us worse off than if our secrets remained hidden. These are the words of a cynical mind, one that sees the darkness long before coming to the light.

In the aftermath of that thought came another: what about all the Samaritans out there? What if people knew how to help us by simply looking at us? What if Adam had known the risk of Eve succumbing to temptation in the garden? Would he have been able to take her hand and lead her to safety? I know there have been a multitude of times that I've sensed someone else's weaknesses, someone else's needs, and walked right past them out of a fear of insulting or judging them by calling them out. Yet in the end, I remained unhelpful, and they remained unhealed. I doubt that's the vision God has for those who are supposed to be His hands and feet to the world around us.

Looking back on that night in the hospital and the day that followed, I see things a little differently. The band on her wrist wasn't an attempt to mock her. It was a confession of a need that enabled others to help her when she was too proud or truly unable to ask for help on her own. I now keep that yellow band in the console of my car so I can see it on a daily basis. It serves as a reminder that I not only need to be willing to admit my own inadequacies, but that I should be mindful of the subtle bracelets each of us wears and how recognizing them on the people I pass every day can better equip me to meet their unspoken needs.

# Chapter Twenty-Two

# Heartbreaking

THE LOOK ON her face was heartbreaking. By ten on Sunday morning, we'd had at least ten doctors flitter through Sam's hospital room. There were general residents, three different neurologists, and the rheumatologist, Dr. Muscal, that we'd been seeing for a year and a half for Samantha's linear morphea. Doctor after doctor evaluated her, each largely repeating the same tests as the doctor before. There were a variety of physical activities to attempt, some of which she could accomplish, until they asked her to stand up and walk around. At that point, they realized that she could only make it about two steps before she lost her balance and needed help. She was annoyed by her loss of coordination and dizziness, but her true frustration was evident when they migrated into the cognitive realm of questioning. She could handle explaining where she was, why she was there, and other queries where the clues around her offered answers; it was probing into her memory that instantly showed something was terribly wrong. She didn't know the month we were in, couldn't recall the alphabet, and even got to the point where her own name was out of reach for her mind. She knew that she should be able to handle everything they were throwing her way with no trouble, but she lacked the ability to recall any of it. With each unanswered question, her own sense of the severity of her affliction grew more pronounced, and tears began to well in her eyes as she realized she simply wasn't herself any more.

As the hours passed, I observed two things about her with which I easily identified. When confronted with the option to admit her own inability or cheat, she would cheat every time. I first noticed it when a doctor asked her to count to five and, for the first time in twenty-four hours, it seemed to be fairly effortless for her. Just as she was saying the words four and five, I noticed her gaze was shifted slightly over the shoulder of the questioning neurologist, directly at the clock on the wall behind her. She could have easily said that she wasn't sure, but instead of admitting her inability, she found a way to convince the people around her that she was just fine and dandy. She did the same thing when another neurologist was manipulating her toes to see if Sam could tell which direction they were being moved. First, already aware of her sneakiness, the physician used his hand to obscure her view, but that didn't prove to be quite enough to trick her. The neurologist smiled, looked over at us, and told us she was cheating by very delicately resisting the direction he was pressing her toe so that she could tell which way he was moving it. I can entirely relate to this approach. I will go to great lengths to prove my own abilities to those around me, glossing over obvious deficits through guise to ensure that no one notices things are amiss. I'm not sure if this is a product of our innate survival instinct (see, I'm already doing it) or if the tie lies more closely with one of the most destructive of sins, pride. Countless verses in the Bible caution us against a path paved with pride, none more intensely than Proverbs 16:5 where it is called an abomination, yet I routinely traverse this road. Some part of me thinks that this time will be different, while at my core, I know that it's only a matter of time before the truth becomes evident once more: I alone am not enough.

The second thing I noticed, as the litany of questions continued unrelenting, is how painful it is to have our failings exposed. Once again, I'm drawn to the simplicity of the story in the Garden of Eden. Here we have man and woman, living in perfect harmony with a single task, tending to the garden. They have virtually no obligations, no one with whom to compete, no distractions from one another, until the serpent enters the picture. We all know the story of the temptation, the fall, but there's a nuance immediately thereafter that I have often overlooked. When the spirit of God moves into that place and finds His two beloved creations cowering in fear, He doesn't immediately punishment them; He calls Adam to confess his sin. Adam must first confront his weakness before restoration can occur. So many of my sins remain in the limbo of my soul, awaiting redemption but are hamstrung by my unwillingness to admit them. As I watch Sam's frustration and defiance build, I can't help but think, the apple didn't fall far from the tree.

# Chapter Twenty-Three

# The Fog

Date: Sunday, 13 January 2013

Hi everyone, I just wanted to send out an update on Sam since so many of you have been asking about her condition and praying for her/us over the last two days. For those of you who weren't aware, Sam has been struggling with severe vertigo since a cold two weeks ago, which has been so intense that she can't walk without help from Beth or me or the support of a wall to run her hand along for extra balance. We'd already seen three or four doctors for that issue, which they felt was a deep inner ear or vestibular nerve problem.

Yesterday morning, while playing a game at breakfast, she suddenly couldn't recite any of the alphabet past the letter C. She didn't know her name, the months of the year, family birthdays, or a number of other things that she's had committed to memory for years. I took her in to Texas Children's, where she underwent both a full brain MRI and a spinal tap to find the cause of her new memory loss issue. On the plus side, the MRI and spinal tap came back perfectly clean, so we've ruled out any types of stroke, tumors, brain inflammation/swelling, or a recurrence and spread of the autoimmune disease she's been battling for the last eighteen months. Knowing none of the causes fit into those buckets is a huge blessing! That said, no one is quite sure what is causing the problem at this point, so we have no solution or treatment plan right now. They are running additional tests on her blood and spinal fluid to check and see if a handful of more exotic viruses could be the cause, so we should hear back on those in a few days. We are also going to get an EEG to check her brain activity and see if that points us in a helpful direction. After a sleepless night at the hospital last night, we are all home tonight to catch up on some much-needed rest.

As you can imagine, Samantha is having a very difficult time with all of this. For those of you who know her, you know that she prides herself on her physical abilities and her intelligence, so having both of those stripped away has been very frustrating for her. We could see the disappointment in her eyes when doctor after doctor asked her questions she knew she should be able to answer, but no answer came. It has been even more upsetting for her because there are plenty of times when she can remember everything, but then it suddenly is no longer accessible to her. At one moment, she was telling me that 39 is the same as one less than eight fives added together, then half an hour later, couldn't count to five without prompting.

Many of you have graciously offered to help, and even more have been praying for her healing and our peace. I can't thank you enough for all of your support. It truly has been incredible, inspiring, and a great source of comfort for us. We would ask that you continue to pray for Sam's well-being, her patience and ours, and a swift road to recovery once we've figured out exactly what we're up against. God has already touched her once in ways that have defied every statistic the doctors provided, so we hold on to the hope that he will do so again.

Love,
Chris

AS THE DAYS pass and no progress is made in arriving at a diagnosis, Sam's memory loss continues to come and go. There are times where it significantly worsens; she's unable to remember anyone's names and can't remember things she heard only a few seconds before. While sitting in her room and playing games together, moments pass where I notice her looking around her as if it's the first time she's ever been there. She hasn't admitted it yet, but I also sometimes see a look of confusion in her eyes when she looks at Beth and me. I have no doubt that in the worst points of her illness, she doesn't know who I am. Yet without knowing my name, she can decipher my role based upon how I have protected and cared for her. In the absence of any history, it is through my behavior that she knows I am her father, and Beth is her mother.

Love is powerful like that—particularly the selfless, sacrificial variety of love. Knowing nothing else, we are able to discern an incredible amount from genuine outpourings of love. I am once again taken to a place where I am the child; He is the father. How many times have I not recognized Him? My mind is often too clouded to recognize His face, no matter how close to me He may be.

The fog that clouds her mind is not unfamiliar to me. I spend many weekend mornings kayaking along the San Jacinto River that runs through my community. I usually head out just as dawn is breaking and slip into the water when it's placid and undisturbed by skiers, boaters, and fishermen. The only sounds that await me are from the animals milling about or the river itself. One morning, I'd made my way to the water earlier than normal, and it was still encompassed in darkness. I slid my kayak in at the boat ramp, climbed aboard, and paddled along the short channel leading to the body of the river. There was nothing noticeably different about that morning, but something in the air didn't feel quite right. I'd been in the water for nearly thirty minutes when I suddenly noticed an eerie absence of sounds. The birds that had been calling only moments before were plunged into complete silence. In the same moment, I felt a cool breeze building behind me, another addition that hasn't been there a minute earlier. I dipped my paddle into the water, held it fast, and let the boat move in a slow 180-degree turn so I was facing upriver. In the predawn light, I could see a blanket of fog steadily moving in my direction. I didn't have time to paddle back to the boat ramp, and it moved quickly enough to overtake me in the

THE FOG

middle of the river. I found the heavy mist to be instantly disorienting. I'd paddled on that river over a hundred times, sometimes in almost complete darkness, and I always knew my way. But when the fog rolled in, I entirely lost my bearings.

It's not as if anything about the river or shoreline had changed. I just couldn't see them any longer. All of the same trees, landmarks, and islands surrounded me, but I lost the ability to make sense of them. Not knowing how long the fog would last, I'd get anxious and clumsily attempt to move one direction or another until I felt sand brushing the bottom of the kayak and knew I'd reached a shore. But even then, I didn't recognize where I was and had no idea how to get back home.

It's hard to imagine that my eight-year-old daughter now feels that way about the face of her family, though I know she does. There are moments where she's improved a little, a sliver of sunlight shining in her eyes. She still can't walk, is still having trouble eating because her tongue isn't working, and remains so dizzy that she uses a belt to strap herself to her chair when we sit down for dinner as a family. Yet when she looks at us and knows who we are and says I love you back to us after we say it to her, it's a little less terrifying. Then the fog rolls in, clouding her mind and blocking her view of everything around her. We are still the people who love her, but she can't see us. This is still the only home she's ever known, but she doesn't recognize it. All I can do is pray for a swift breeze and sunlight to push the darkness away. I pray and pray and pray.

# Chapter Twenty-Four

# The Battle That Never Was

Date: Wednesday, 16 January 2013

We once again wanted to thank everyone for all of the wonderful prayers, gifts, cards, gift certificates to restaurants (awesome!), and help we've been getting lately. We didn't want to set up a care calendar because we aren't really sure what our schedule will be like since we're making frequent trips to a slew of doctors. Even though we haven't been able to see you guys in person very much, we want you to know not just how helpful but also how positive it's kept us. The days (and nights) have been pretty long lately, so all of the encouragement has been amazing.

Last Monday, we took Samantha in for the EEG we mentioned, and the results all came back within normal ranges, so we are still no closer to having a diagnosis for her; we are just able to rule out a few other potential causes. We did find out that she's sensitive to being over stimulated; after the strobe light portion of the EEG, she was incredibly off-balance and reverted to talking and acting like an eighteen-month-old. She was afraid of everyone getting burned by hot plates at dinner, kept talking about monsters when she saw shadows, and insisted on falling asleep with her light on, which she's never done in her life. With enough sleep and downtime, she does much better with her balance and acts more like herself, but her memory is still not where it should be. We have started physical therapy, which we're doing twice a week, to help overcome some of her balance issues, and she was actually walking well on her own for most of the day. Unfortunately, doing too many of the exercises triggers her vertigo, and it gets intense enough to make her see double and start to act like she's several years younger than she is again.

We are still waiting on results from a panel of blood and spinal fluid tests for some exotic viruses that now seem to be the most likely cause, but the doctors are still at a loss to explain all of her symptoms. We continue to praise God for all of the truly scary things that we've been able to rule out through the myriad of tests she's endured. It might seem crazy to say this, but we are inexplicably calm and peaceful in the midst of this time of confusion and absence of answers, and we can attribute that to nothing but the encouragement and prayers we have received from all of you.

Please continue to pray for us to have patience; we never know what version of Samantha we're going to get, and some of them can be incredibly intense, so it has been very exhausting. Also, please keep praying for her, she's getting very frustrated with herself for not remembering her name, birthday, and tons of other things that normally require no thought at all for her. We are trying to keep the perspective that this affords us an opportunity to teach her new things every day, but we're definitely ready to have our little girl back.

Thank you for everything,

Chris and Beth

1 Thessalonians 5:11—"Therefore encourage one another and build each other up, just as in fact you are doing."

AS I WRITE this chapter, my wife and I are approaching our fourteenth wedding anniversary. For those who have been in a relationship for that amount of time, you're wildly familiar with the petty arguments that arise over the course of nearly a decade and a half. Looking back, I marvel at the trivial things over which we'll argue. From disagreements about who left a cup in the living room, whose turn it is to wash dishes, who forgot to bring the snacks during a long car ride—it's seemingly never ending.

I remember our first trip as more than husband and wife when my daughter was a mere eight months old. My parents had a timeshare that secured them one week at a hotel on the Hawaiian island of Kauai, but for some reason, they weren't going to be able to use it. As it turned out, not only was it a free week, but it was a free week for a two-bedroom suite. I failed to mention earlier; during Sam's infancy and the period of colic that ran until she was about twelve weeks old, two of Beth's cousins, Lyla and Katie, had been a godsend. Though they lived three hours away in Austin and were both gainfully employed, they drove down to Houston on the weekends to watch Samantha at night and give Beth and me a chance to catch up on some much needed sleep. We'd been wondering how we could repay them, so when the chance to invite them to join us on a trip to Hawaii came around, it was too perfect to pass up. Even though Samantha was still quite young, we decided that an opportunity like that might not arise again anytime soon, and we were going to jump on it.

When the date for the trip rolled around, we couldn't have been more excited. Lyla and Katie drove down to spend the night, and early the next morning, we made our way to the airport to start our adventure. You know the routine—finding a parking place, checking in for the flight, clearing security, navigating Houston's substantial George Bush Intercontinental Airport, grabbing a bite to eat, and counting down the minutes before boarding the plane. Once the time until boarding dwindled enough, we decided it would be a good idea to change Samantha's diaper. After all, it was going to be a very long flight, so we wanted to keep her as comfortable as possible. Beth offered to handle the changing and asked me where I'd put the diaper bag. I politely responded that I'd not put it anywhere; it must have been where she was sitting, and she'd simply forgotten she had it. That's when we came to a painful realization: we didn't have the diaper bag. In our haste to get to the airport that morning, we'd both overlooked it and left it at the house. The diaper bag was stuffed with everything we needed for the flight. Diapers, pacifiers, food, blankets, and all of the other modern accoutrements associated with keeping a child alive (and hopefully silent) on a plane for eight hours. With an impossibly limited window of time, we agreed that there was only one option: I had to go get it.

While I am fairly respectful of rules, laws, and the safety of those around me, this wasn't one of my finer moments as a considerate citizen. I was jumping down staircases in the parking garage, sliding across the hood of my car, and pretending traffic lights shifting from yellow to red simply meant to speed up. I'm not sure what the land speed record is in a Toyota Camry, but I'm pretty sure I broke it at least three times as I raced back to the house, got the diaper bag, and made it back to the airport. I had to go through security again, make it to the distant gate again, and literally ran up to the plane as they were preparing to close the door and leave our posse behind. But I'd made it, and we all celebrated as we boarded the plane, ignoring the condescending stares of the flight attendants and passengers around us. Once we'd settled in, the jubilance subsided, and my wife and I looked at each other, more than ready to lay blame for who was responsible for the chaotic start to our blissful week of relaxation. To say it was a short-lived discussion would be wildly untrue. Obviously, it was her fault, and she still has trouble admitting that, but I forgive her. When she writes a book, she can blame me.

During the period of Samantha's most recent illness, with sleep deprivation running rampant and no solutions for her worsening condition, you can imagine how easy it would be to argue about everything. Now imagine not disagreeing about who left a diaper bag at the house before a vacation but being conflicted about the nature of God and whether or not He allows children to suffer or causes them to suffer. Think about what it would be like to be polarized on elements of theology and faith at a time when your children are searching for answers to the same questions you're debating as adults.

I can still remember the look on Samantha's face when she said, she didn't understand why God would make her sick and what lesson she was supposed to learn from it, a sentiment that echoed Beth's thought process. I knelt next to Sam's bed and explained that some people believed that, while others felt that the nature of God didn't require Him to use painful things to accomplish His will. In the midst of trying circumstances in life, God remains hopeful that we will turn bad experiences into good ones and remain faithful through it all. Beth and I agreed that all things happen for a reason, but we didn't see eye to eye on the causes of those things.

What was truly amazing, however, was that we never really fought about it. How foolish would God have found us to be had we truly battled about His nature? We discussed, we disagreed, we deliberated, but we once again found ourselves oddly at peace as a couple in a time when the stress of the situation around us should have rendered us anything but calm and accepting of our differences. No matter what the cause, we felt the hand of God in our relationship and were reassured that all would be well. We knew not what that meant in terms of healing or timing, just that it would ultimately be so, and our faith, Samantha's included, would remain undiminished.

THE BATTLE THAT NEVER WAS

# Chapter Twenty-Five

# I Am

Date: Thursday, 24 January 2013
Hi everyone,

We wanted to give everyone another update after today's visit with the neurologists at Texas Children's. All of the blood and spinal fluid tests have come back, and none of them bring us any closer to a diagnosis for her condition. Again, we have ruled out a lot of options, but nothing definitive has emerged. As of right now, they are still sticking with the theory that she has some sort of virus that is affecting her brain and causing the myriad of problems she's had over the last month. We discussed taking an aggressive approach and giving her steroids to try and accelerate the healing process, even without a firm diagnosis, but we all agreed that we'd rather not do that given that she's started to show some signs of improvement on her own. If any of you recall her on steroids about a year ago, it wasn't pretty at all! Don't let anyone tell you 'roid rage is a myth; it's real, and she had it full-on.

As for how she's doing, fortunately, her vertigo has finally disappeared, which has been great for lifting her spirits since she's literally been either sitting still or crawling around the house for a few weeks. This morning, she was doing roundoffs and practicing front flips, so her mobility is wildly improved. Unfortunately, in place of the vertigo, she is now having difficulty with numbness and tingling, mostly in her right leg, but at times in all of her extremities. She is also still having some fairly dramatic mood swings and memory loss, though both of those have gotten a bit better in the last couple of days. When the day started today, she didn't know the alphabet or how to write over half of the letters; then an hour and a half later, she was playing a board game with me, reading every card on her own with no problem, and remembering answers to questions she only saw once about a month ago. The neurologists feel that her brain is likely recovering from whatever afflicted her and that it will just take time for it to power all the way back up. Sam was very excited to hear that they are encouraging her to try and start back into her normal routine soon, with the hope that being back in school for an hour or two a day (as early as Monday) and back in gymnastics (probably a week from Monday) will help her mind revert to how it was before her illness. You can imagine our collective relief when they said that to us!

We also wanted to say thank you once more to everyone. The outpouring of help, support, and prayer has truly been beyond measure. It seems that I can't go anywhere without hearing that people are praying for Samantha's healing, which has been an incredible blessing and source of comfort during this trial. Her spirit also remains entirely unbroken. As we were driving home from the doctor today, she told me that the first letter of her best friend's name started with a *G*. After I couldn't figure it out with a couple of guesses, she told me God was the name of her best friend. I was a bit faster on the uptake when she told me *J* was the first letter of her next best friend's name, and Beth and I were perfectly happy to be behind those two on her list.

To have a child enduring such hardship but remaining joyful, faithful, and moving down a path of healing with no help from physicians is a beautiful gift, and I wholeheartedly believe that we have your prayers to thank for that.

Thank you,
Chris and Beth

Psalm 52:9—For what you have done I will always praise you in the presence of your faithful people. And I will hope in your name, for your name is good.

AFTER THE FIRST night in the hospital, there was an inkling of sleep deprivation spreading through the family. We slept for three hours tops, but with nurses coming in to take blood pressure, Samantha crying about the discomfort of her IV, and the endless sounds that echo through hospitals at night, the little sleep we had didn't leave any of us well rested. In the nights that followed, sleep deprivation became a common theme. Samantha's condition worsened, and she was continually experiencing new symptoms. One day, she'd have virtually no use of her legs, and another day, she would complain that it felt like pins and needles were stabbing along her extremities. While the physical symptoms were always a cause for concern, the most troublesome issues were when her mental capacity was impacted. With increasing frequency, she would wake up, talking as if she was not an eight-year-old but a fifteen-month-old, terrified of shadows, insisting on chewing straws all night, and throwing violent temper tantrums at the drop of a hat. As I was putting her to sleep during one of these episodes, the following conversation ensued.

"Sammy, it's time for you to get in bed and get some rest," I said.

"No. Not tired," she defiantly replied through drooping eyelids.

"Yes, kiddo, you are." I picked her up and carried her slowly to her bed, trying not to rouse her or exacerbate her dizziness. "If you get some sleep, you will wake up feeling a little bit better in the morning."

"Not sleepy. Want to stay awake. Want to play." Her volume was increasing, the focus of her sleepy eyes growing more intense.

"No, ma'am, we aren't going to play. We are all going to sleep."

"You go to sleep, I stay awake. I be reaaaaaally quiet." She was now looking at me through a tiny gap she'd created using her index finger and thumb to show me just how small the sound would be.

My head swung left to right. "If you stay up and play, you'll keep your brother awake, and he needs his rest too." Generally, her level of compassion for her brother would serve as a source of regulation for issues like this, but she wasn't herself, so it fell on deaf ears.

By now, she was in her own world, ignoring me entirely, her brow furrowed, and her eyes darted back and forth as she struggled to escape being put to sleep. Then her scowl flattened and reversed; her face suddenly beaming with a bright smile. "I go outside to play with dog! You go to sleep, I go outside, I no wake No-No up." She was practically clapping for herself at this point, using the name she'd made up for

Noah when she couldn't recall his full name, and was convinced that she'd put her plan into action the moment I set her down.

I took a long, slow breath and returned to the dialogue that continued for several minutes before it spiraled into a furious battle. Her frustrated screams lasted nearly half an hour as she continually jumped out of bed and tried to run downstairs again and again. Each time, I would scoop her up, put her back in her room, and stand outside of her door until she came bolting out again. Eventually, she realized it was a fight she wouldn't win, so she climbed into bed, crying with rage at my obvious insolence until she finally fell asleep.

That night, the seed of her trying to leave the house was planted in my mind, and it didn't take long until it blossomed into serious concern. The issue wasn't so much that she'd get outside undetected; the alarm would sound, so I'd know the moment she opened a door or window. I was worried about her trying to navigate the stairs by herself. Her balance was still questionable at best, but she'd also developed issues with her limbs not functioning properly, making walking nearly impossible and descending stairs a very dangerous proposition. In the end, remaining vigilant to protect her from herself trumped my own sense of comfort and need for sleep. That night was the first of many that I spent sleeping on a mattress between her bedroom and the staircase.

In the weeks that followed, my level of sleep deprivation ran rampant. I can function without exhaustion, illness, or having a bad temperament with a few hours of sleep a night, but that's when I'm controlling what those hours are and when there's a period with at least an hour and a half of uninterrupted sleep. Lying on a mattress in the middle of a living room with my mind trained to wake at the slightest sound to ensure Sam didn't slip past me undetected, the number of hours passed in restful sleep dwindled to virtually zero. My sense of time became warped, with nights passing in what seemed like an eternity at some times and in a matter of minutes at others. At first, I attempted to spend the hours in prayerful meditation, but focusing grew more and more difficult as the days passed. Instead, I found that I viewed the hours as wasted if I didn't try to figure out what was happening to Samantha. We still had no diagnosis despite the battery of tests. So to make use of the time, I simply decided that I wasn't going to sleep. I might as well keep myself awake and spend those hours each night researching, checking to be sure she wasn't having seizures (a symptom

I AM

the neurologists expected her to develop), and searching for a solution. Just as with her other illness eighteen months earlier, I thought that if I looked at it hard enough, spoke with enough doctors, read enough articles, and journals—if I tried hard enough, I'd find a way to fix her. Then I remembered two words from the Bible and, once again, found myself more at ease. The words are simple, yet profound, found in Exodus 3:14, "I am."

God says these words to Moses, and it's echoed in John 8:58 when Jesus says the same thing to demonstrate that He is intimately entwined with the God of the Old Testament. This is the kind of statement that was deemed heretical to the legalistic Jews of that day. Yet the same words that confused a terrified man in the Old Testament and set the stage for a crucifixion in the New Testament provided me with a reminder that my sense of time is irrelevant in the big picture. He didn't say "I was," nor did He profess "I will be." He simply said "I am." God resides beyond the hands of a watch, and His plan will be made known according to His schedule, not mine. I realized that the more I fixated on finding a solution, the more I tried to squeeze as many seconds out of a night as possible, the more my sense of time was warped by sleep deprivation, the further from Him I drifted. As I sat in the midst of my self-created sea of sleeplessness, His voice called out to the tempest and calmed the treacherous waters with a mere two words, "I am."

# Chapter Twenty-Six

# Nowhere to Be Found

I'M STANDING IN the darkness; my forearms starting to burn with fatigue from gripping a doorknob for the last forty-five minutes, and Samantha is nowhere to be found. Make no mistake, there's a child on the other side of the door, but it's no longer the little girl I know.

The illness that's taken hold of her mind has stripped away so much of who she is. Her athleticism, brilliance, quick wit, and unending desire to take care of other people are gone. Any semblance of compassion, confidence, or affection has vanished, and what remains is a violent, terrified, incoherent creature whose feet and fists have been hammering at the walls and door of her room for what's approaching an hour. Every few minutes, she'll turn on her light; I'll open the door to turn it off, forcefully put her back in bed, and then shut the door before she's able to dash through it to escape. She shrieks with fury at this captivity, but since her mind can't find words now, most of the sounds I hear are animalistic distortions of her normally sweet voice. Words can't describe the pain I feel during this new nightly routine, but the memory of a recent night fills my mind in the midst of the shouting.

We don't have the kind of house where you'll ever hear the words "wait until your dad gets home" as it relates to discipline. In fact, for one Mother's Day in the past, I made Beth a wooden sign of her favorite Bible verse from Proverbs 23:13, "Do not withhold discipline from a child; if you punish them with the rod, they will not die." Needless to say, she can hold her own when it comes to handling the kids. While I go to great lengths to protect her from the emotional trauma of caring for Samantha when she's in this state, Beth feels it's her responsibility as a mother and the queen of our humble castle to take an active role in watching over her daughter. One night, when she insisted on waging the inevitable war of putting Sam to sleep, I left to work out and returned to a quiet house an hour and a half later, which I thought was a good sign.

I made my way to our room and found Beth sitting on the bed with the left side of her face obscured by a hand resting along the underside of her jaw. I could see that she'd been crying, but when she turned to face me, I saw that one of her eyes wasn't just red and puffy from tears; it was swollen and already growing black underneath. In a muffled voice, she told me that when she'd gone in to turn off the light for the twenty-fifth time that night and put Samantha back in bed in the darkness, Sam kicked violently, and her heel collided with Beth's left jaw.

When Beth gets hurt, she generally wants to be left alone, so it was a near-silent night until she fell asleep, and I went to play sentry, sleeping on my makeshift bed at the top of the stairs. It wasn't until the next morning when she attempted to take a bite of breakfast that she heard an audible pop as her jaw slid back into alignment. Unbeknownst to me, Sam's kick landed with enough force to shift Beth's jaw out of place, but Beth didn't want to upset me by sharing that minor detail. And I think I'm the tough one . . .

I'm brought out of the memory and back into the present when I feel the full weight of Sam's body slam into the door. I hear her nails raking across it in a primal fashion before she retreats, only to careen into it again a few seconds later. With her first illness, I'd have grown increasingly enraged and concerned as the minutes dredged on, but I now try to guide my mind to a place where I can search for God's presence. Like the night we spent in the emergency room in early January, my perspective of the circumstance changes; instead of seeing her battling me, I see myself battling Him. I hear and feel her through the door and think of all the times I'm overtaken by a vehemently rebellious spirit and lash out as He tries to contain me and prevent me from harming myself and those around me. In His compassion, He hems me in and waits for the flame of evil within me to burn out.

If we search the Bible, illnesses of the mind were often attributed to demonic possession. Saul is seized by a harmful spirit in 1 Samuel 19 when he lashes out at David with inexplicable violence. In Matthew 9 and 12, we see men possessed by demons, whose sight and speech failed them. Mark 5 describes a man so overcome by unclean spirits that he walked for years through a graveyard he'd made his home. Because of the legion within him, he possessed such otherworldly strength that no chains could bind him; he cried out day and night and cut himself with stones until Jesus arrived and cleansed him. In reading about the disease the neurologists believe afflicts Samantha, some connections have been suggested between historical records of possessions and anti-NMDA autoimmune encephalitis. Changes in gait, the inability to speak, hallucinations, paranoia, irrational fears, uncanny strength, vocal distortions, and many other common threads exist. I'm not suggesting she's been overtaken in that way; I don't have the wisdom to discern between evil and illness. I only see how far she's fallen from what she once was and wonder what the cause may be.

I pray for Samantha to return to us and for a renewal of my patience as time crawls past. I pray for Beth to be willing to let me carry this weight so she doesn't have to and for my son's peace of mind as he hears his sister's screams echo through the house. I try to pray loudly enough to drown out the sounds of this struggle and wait with hope for the tranquility of silence to fall over us all.

# Chapter Twenty-Seven

# Desensitized

Date: Friday, 1 February 2013

It's hard to believe that it's only been a week since we sent the e-mail below. Since last Thursday, Samantha has improved dramatically. She went to school every day this week for about two hours and, although she was tired by the time she came home each day, her memory has come rushing back into focus. She's gone from being unable to repeat the alphabet in English this time last week to making a perfect score on a spelling test for ten English and ten Spanish vocabulary words today. With her memory coming back, she is far less frustrated, so her mood has improved too. She is still periodically dizzy, but if she sits still for a while or takes a quick nap, it goes away in short order. She is also still complaining about pain in one of her ankles, which we thought was related to her illness, but we now think that she may have twisted or sprained her ankle doing gymnastics at home when she couldn't feel her legs last week. Physically, she is also doing incredibly well; we actually just got home from an hour-long gymnastics class where she had a great time. Again, to go from being unable to walk two weeks ago to doing front flips and handstands today is absolutely amazing. Her only major complaint at this point is that she's having fairly intense nightmares, but she understands that her mind is just creating images that aren't real, and she's falling back to sleep without much trouble.

We have another neurology appointment on Thursday for them to assess her, so we can't wait to show off her amazing improvement. Her condition remains undiagnosed, but as we told the doctors from the onset, we don't care what it is; we just want her to be herself again. They will no doubt continue to struggle to put her illness and recovery into medical terms, but we know from the bottom of our hearts that her healing lies beyond what mere medicine can define. We once again want to thank everyone for the multitude of prayers, assistance, and compassion over the last six weeks. We truly couldn't have made it through this period of concern and uncertainty with the patience and perseverance that we've experienced without you.

Enjoy your weekend,

Chris and Beth

A S THE DAYS trudged on, we finally saw an improvement in a few aspects of Sam's condition. The vertigo that had persisted for nearly a month started to abate and would only come in full force if she was lying down or at seemingly random times throughout the day. She was absolutely elated at some modicum of healing—even if other symptoms persisted, and new ones continued to plague her. As an example of newly emerging issues, one Saturday morning, she was sitting on her brother's bed, her legs dangling over the edge. Noah was explaining pictures in a book to her because she was having trouble seeing them, which was another symptom that had already lasted several weeks. While she was distracted, I reached over and used my fingertips to tickle the sole of her left foot, but she seemed not to notice at all. I switched to her right foot, repeated the tickling, and she instantly pulled her foot back, looking over at me with a grin. When she was focused on the book again, I moved back to her left foot and went past tickling to pushing, gently scratching, and ultimately pinching, all with zero response.

I stepped out of the room, made my way downstairs, and picked up the phone to speak with the on-call neurologist at Texas Children's. I assumed she'd need to come in and get checked out again since that was a fairly serious new symptom, but I was relieved when the physician confessed that they'd already run every test they could think of, so bringing her in was unlikely to accomplish anything. He told me to keep an eye on her, ensure it was only an issue with her extremities, and to let them know if things worsened or migrated away from her hands and feet. The candor of that exchange was surprising and strangely comforting.

When I hung up the phone, I heard something I'd not heard for over a month: the sound of a firmly landed cartwheel echoing through the rafters overhead. Since her illness began, she'd been too dizzy to do the gymnastics she loved; but she was apparently feeling well enough to start again, and I couldn't help but smile. I made my way upstairs to find Sam and Noah both taking turns doing cartwheels on two gymnastics mats they'd spread out on the floor, occasionally using the mattress I'd been sleeping on in the middle of the room as their final landing place. It didn't take long for the gymnastics to turn into a wrestling match, and they joined forces to try to take me down. In the melee that ensued, I had Noah pinned on the ground, and Samantha stepped in front of me, her body twisted to the side, and she firmly landed a kick on my shoulder with her right foot. Ever the calculator, she grinned, pivoted to balance on her right foot, and then spun around to kick me in the other shoulder with her left foot as hard as she possibly could. Shocked by her use of force, I asked her why she kicked me that hard and warned that she might hurt herself against the resilience of my rock-hard muscles (for those of you who know me, stop laughing). In response to my question, she just smiled and said that since she couldn't feel anything in that leg, she could kick me as hard as she wanted, and it wouldn't matter. The numbness afforded her a freedom to act in ways that she otherwise couldn't, and she enjoyed exercising that unrestrained ability to let loose.

I think that the loss of sensation is one of the most perilous and rapidly growing facets of our increasingly detached culture. Kids are watching things well beyond their depth; sensationalism is rampant, and the advent of access to online videos of everything your mind can imagine creates an anonymous playground for those who turn a blind eye to the true nature of what they are seeing.

As a kid, I prided myself on my ability to shut down my sensory perception anytime I wanted. It wasn't an easily acquired skill, but at my "peak," I could drown out nearly anything, thanks to my trips to the neighborhood swimming pool. Growing up on the southwest side of Houston, there were only a couple of pools on the block, mostly at the homes of older couples whose kids had moved out, which meant invites to hit the water were few and far between. Taking a dip required walking or biking a dozen blocks to the neighborhood pool, which is where most kids in the area congregated to pass time when school was out. In Houston, the heat and humidity of the summer months grow so oppressive that there really aren't many options other than a pool for those wanting to get out of the house for a bit. Needless to say, the pool was always packed.

Even in those days, I wasn't much of a crowd person. I didn't care for the shouting, shrieking, and bumping into one another that a more extroverted kid would thrive on. There were times when the stimulation grew too great, and to escape it, I would dive to the bottom of the deep end and sit for as long as I could. The pool was thirteen feet deep, so for a kid of my size and age to swim down to the bottom was odd enough, but to be able to hold my breath for better than a minute and

DESENSITIZED

sit motionless on the drain left more than one lifeguard rather uneasy. Their concern, in my mind, was just that—theirs. I was far more focused on easing my own frustration, so it became something of a habit. I found solitude and peace in being immersed in the water; it was an incredible escape from all that surrounded me. Everyone was still screaming, running around, and shoving each other, but I was immune to it. I could still occasionally hear faint echoes of their actions, but for the most part, they ceased to exist, and I was alone with nothing but the sound of my own heartbeat to keep me company.

In time, I learned to make use of that skill without being enveloped in an aqueous sanctuary; I could do it anytime, anyplace. If the shouts of the teachers disappointed in my behavior grew too loud, I'd internally silence them. If an argument between my parents was overly intense, I could make it disappear with an increasingly limited effort.

The whole mind-over-matter thing was pretty big in the '80s, so I was wildly impressed with my ever-improving skill set in that realm. Naturally, I wanted to test the limits of my abilities and continually found new ways to push the envelope. What if I could tune out sights, not just sounds? What if I could dial down my awareness of pain? The possibilities were limitless, and I was hungry to see just how far I could go. A bit disturbingly, I found that pain was easier than expected to filter out. I would typically start small, but things always progressed into more dangerous territory. Perhaps it would begin as getting my hand near a flame to see how long I could handle it. The next step would be putting the flame out with my fingertips. After that came ever-increasing temperatures until I was even foolish enough to pull things out of the oven with nothing but my bare hands.

During the years that I tested this aspect of my awareness, my body was covered with cuts and bruises, and I broke an alarming number of bones. I'd decide that jumping down an entire flight of concrete stairs was a good idea and snap a couple of bones in my foot. Some friends and I would climb up the fire escape to the roof of a two-story building and, as they looked over the side wondering how far down it was, I'd come flying past them, leaping down to the ground with a shout of thrilled excitement. I might even have been foolish enough to want to know how it would feel to go backward off of a cliff into a pile of leaves ten feet down, only to miss the pile entirely and drop an extra ten feet before landing on the bank of a river with one arm behind me. But by then, I'd gotten so adept at tucking away the sensation of pain that I went three days before going to a doctor, who was floored when he saw that the X-ray film displayed an obviously broken humerus. I'd snapped clean through the bone in my upper arm; my fascia, muscles, and tendons were the only things holding it in place, and it simply didn't hurt.

It's funny how my greatest strength can be taken to such an extreme that it becomes my biggest weakness. As a Christian, empathy and compassion are supposed to be fundamental elements of my faith. When Jesus is asked about the most important commandment in Matthew 22, His response is to love God and to love your neighbors. How can I possibly love them if I feel nothing for them? In another example of Christ's compassion for the suffering of others, we find in John 11:35, "Jesus wept." For those of you who have to memorize a verse for some reason and want a shortcut, John 11:35 has the illustrious title of the shortest verse in the Bible, so keep that in mind. In this instance, Jesus is trying to comfort the sisters of Lazarus, who are weeping after the loss of their brother. Moved by their anguish, Jesus uses that compassion to perform one of his most miraculous feats when he raises Lazarus from the dead.

I try to think about the miracles that could be accomplished through me if I will just allow myself to feel everything around me. If I thought of the needs of others before myself, how many lives could be touched by God's grace, forgiveness, and compassion moving through me? Even for someone who has deadened and desensitized himself, when I fully accept God's love for me, I feel compelled to make my way to the surface and share that love with the people around me.

## Chapter Twenty-Eight

# Little Man

MY SON, NOAH, has matured into an incredible young man over the last two years. When Samantha's first illness began, he was a mere four years old. He knew something was wrong with his sister and knew that she had to see a lot of doctors. He witnessed some of her post-treatment exhaustion, mood swings, and rage, but the depth of what plagued her was obviously beyond his ability to understand.

During her battle with morphea, he displayed compassion and kindness; but she never truly slowed down, so he didn't get to show the depth of his love during that time. With the affliction that hit full force this January, the same can't be said. Since her symptoms changed without warning every day, he had to be prepared to handle various versions of his sister. A handful of moments stand out that remind me of the purity of love that children can display, and the strength that the seemingly weak amongst us can muster that overpowers us all.

The first thing I remember is something I'd expect from concerned parents in times such as those; he feared for his sister's well-being. He'd known she was sick around Christmas and had witnessed her issues with balance that hadn't abated after two weeks of dizziness and vision problems. On the morning of January 12, however, he knew things worsened dramatically. He was sitting across the table from her at breakfast when her memory seemingly evaporated before our eyes. He watched me as I calmly questioned her, probing to find out just how deep her memory loss ran, and he knew something was seriously wrong when we walked out of a restaurant with breakfast partially uneaten (I'm known as "trash can" in our house for my ability to eat my food, plus everyone else's) so that I could drop him off at home and immediately take Samantha to the emergency room. His eyes were moist with tears as I called Beth and told her to pack a bag with drinks, snacks, books, and games to take to the hospital since I anticipated being there for most of the day. Beth and I spoke in the most grown-up words we could summon as I tried to explain how Samantha was behaving and express my thoughts on potential causes. While we expected him to have his own concerns, we both hoped he would assume she was going to be perfectly fine, just as she ultimately had been with her morphea. As Sam and I left the house, Noah waved to us from the back door as we pulled out of the driveway, obvious concern weighing heavily on his normally smile-filled face. When Beth started to gather together a few things for his trip to play with friends, he stopped her to ask her a question I mentioned several chapters ago. "Mom, is Samantha going to die?" As I drove into the hospital, I was foolish enough to think that bringing Sam into the ER that morning was going to be the hardest of the jobs Beth or I would have that day.

Noah intuitively grasped the gravity of the situation, pushed through our attempts to veil its severity, and cut to the core with six simple words. Later that night, in the darkness of the hospital room in which we slept, I remember wondering if some part of the little boy in him was broken that day as he was forced to wrestle with fears he was too young to handle. I hoped he had been reassured by Beth's response that Samantha was going to be fine and by his conviction that his sister was too strong to let anything defeat her, but I worried about the happiness in his little heart nonetheless.

The second time that he showed strength well beyond his years was a few weeks later. Our home is a veritable madhouse most of the time, with both of our kids being extremely physically active. Waking to the sounds of crashing, jumping, or some form of ruckus is part of our daily routine. In the latter part of December and first part of January, mornings had become eerily silent. Then, one morning, I heard the familiar ceiling-shaking reverberations of a full-on collision, followed by infectious laughter. Before I could finish what I was doing in the kitchen, I heard the same crash and cackling a few more times.

When I went upstairs to find the source of that sorely missed euphony, a part of me leapt at the possibility that Samantha had simply woken up no longer feeling dizzy or unsteady. As the kids came into view, however, I realized that the next best thing was happening. Noah was standing up in the middle of an open game room, with a full-sized gymnastics mat between him and the doorway to an adjoining room. At the count of three, Sam came flying through the doorway at full speed, lost her balance just as she made it to the place Noah was standing, and slammed into the mat with such force that Noah was hurled backward onto a couch, and she came crashing down on top of the mat. Her dizziness was just as pronounced as it had been the day before, but when she started to express her frustration at her inability, Noah suggested they find a way to play a game where she only needed to walk four or five steps at a time. He measured out that distance, shielded himself with the mat, and with a bit of a challenge in his voice, beckoned her to come at him with everything she had. He didn't focus on her inability but found a way to make her limitations fit into the construct of what could be accomplished and remind her that she was still the strong one in their relationship. In the midst of her illness, he manifested the message of Romans 5:3, pushing her to persevere through her tribulations, reminding her of her true character and, above all, giving her hope that she wouldn't be reduced to someone who needed anyone else's help. Her vision was still askew, so she had trouble focusing on me when I finally stepped out from my hiding place, but the smile on her face stretched from ear to ear because of what he had done to remind her of who she was at her core.

The most memorable point where Noah displayed strength beyond what I believed to be possible for a five-year-old was the weekend after Sam's trip to the ER. I'd not been sleeping much since I was expecting her to develop seizures at some point, and I began each morning with a hopeful prayer that Sam would start to experience healing, only to be let down far more often than not. Her dizziness remained potent enough to render her mobility questionable, though she had adapted by crawling from one place to the next to avoid relying on her unsteady gait. Her vision was also distorted, with words either blurred or moving, so most of the games we played on a routine basis were also out of the question. Her days largely consisted of sitting with Noah, watching him play, and joining in whenever she was able. Just after seven that Saturday morning, I made my way upstairs to check and see how she was doing and was met with a vision I still have trouble articulating without tears of pride welling up in my eyes.

I ascended the staircase quietly, made the 180 degree–turn at the top of the railing to face Noah's room, and saw the rectangular ribbon of light framing his closed door that told me he was already awake for the day. I pushed his door open and found the room illuminated but empty. The door leading toward his bathroom and his sister's room was standing open, and the silhouettes of their two bodies pressed together came into view. They were moving through the door of her room, heading to his, but when Samantha woke that morning, her legs and hands weren't functioning at all. She couldn't stand, couldn't walk, and couldn't crawl on her own. Instead of running like a frightened child to find me and get me to help her, my son gently pulled her to the edge of her bed, had her slip an arm over his shoulders, and carried his big sister from her bedroom into his. I stepped slowly back until I was just out of view and watched as he set her on his bed, handed her a stuffed animal she'd pointed to but was unable to speak well enough to request, and pulled some toys for himself onto his bed where they sat shoulder to shoulder to play quietly together.

Part of my mind instantly started to catalogue some of her new symptoms from those few seconds, but it was quieted by the stronger voice pushing through, reminding me that I was witnessing a love so pure that tainting it with thought was entirely out of the question. My son clearly expected nothing from her in return for his kindness, nor did he anticipate witnesses to his act of compassion, yet he behaved as most of us do only if we think the entire world is watching, and an award is waiting in the wings. Just as we read in 1 Kings 19, Elijah feels the presence of God, not in the blustering wind, tremulous earthquake or incendiary fire, but in the near-silent gentleness of a zephyr. I so often expect displays of love and affection to manifest themselves in dramatic ways, but it was in the silence of a moment that I witnessed a love too perfect to be anything other than divinely inspired.

Perhaps I was right that night in the hospital; maybe a part of the little boy was left behind when Noah wondered whether or not his sister would survive her new ordeal. But much like my first fears with Samantha, I was a fool to think that what was happening would somehow break his spirit or leave him weaker than he'd been before. For a couple of years now, when I leave for work, I remind him to take care of our girls because he's the man of the house when I'm not there; that statement has never been truer than it is now, and I couldn't be prouder of how he has grown through all of this. The little boy wasn't broken; he was simply given a choice between maturing or not. By the grace of God, he chose the path less traveled by, and in the months that have followed, that has made all the difference.

# Chapter Twenty-Nine

# Against All Odds

A COUPLE OF YEARS ago, my family attended a concert where Brandon Heath and Britt Nicole were performing. Both are incredibly talented writers, performers, and storytellers, often painting the picture of a song with a tale of its origin as they strum its introductory chords. At one point in the concert, Brandon told the story of a particular tune, wanting to point out that God speaks to us in ways that can only be done by one who truly knows us. Being in Houston, Brandon thought it appropriate to confess an obsession with all things NASA. He'd been a geek about space and astronauts for as long as he could remember, dreaming of traveling to far off places since boyhood. He went on to share a tradition that takes place when the shuttle is in orbit. During the morning check-in with shuttle command in Houston, each astronaut gets a little bit of airtime to play a song and wake everyone on the mission up when the day begins. During one mission, a song of his was chosen to start the day. In his mind, that was pretty neat, a cool coincidence that he took note of but didn't find particularly incredible. It was a friend who pointed out the gravity of that moment to him: God chose his dorky, unknown obsession to communicate His love. A song Brandon wrote was playing in the one place he had always dreamt of being, and viewed in that light, it was a uniquely beautiful thing.

I have already mentioned: I am a bit of a math nerd. And yes, using the words "a bit" is an intentional understatement. On my nightstand, you'll find a sudoku book or two, a Rubik's cube, texts on code breaking, and other evidence of how deep the vein of math runs in me. In school, I enjoyed and excelled in math courses and, at work, had a boss that once abstained from bringing a calculator into meetings because she said that if she had me there, she didn't need anything else. That's definitely an exaggeration, but you get the idea.

I even had an economics course in college where I said that anything and everything could be broken down into math.

Can you explain decisions with math? "Yes, it's just a matter of adding up the good, and weighing it against the bad of a given set of actions. If the goods . . ."

Can you show how people fall in love with math? "Yes, the feelings people experience are just a mix of chemicals that affect your body . . ."

Eventually, we arrived at what they viewed as the difficult question of whether or not the value of a human life could be quantified. The professor smiled, looked in my direction, and my response began. "Of course, wrongful death lawsuits do it all the time. You take the value of wages that would have been earned multiplied by the difference in the lifespan at death relative to average lifespan . . ."

Theologically, it isn't that I view math as having some degree of superiority over God; I think it is His structure for the design and function of everything around and within us. That sentiment is echoed in the book *The Language of God: A Scientist Presents Evidence for Belief* by world-renowned geneticist, Francis Collins, who led the project to sequence the human genome in the late '90s.

Samantha's first illness is incredibly rare, happening so infrequently that med students came in to see her during visits since they'd likely not see a case like hers again during their time on dermatologic rotation. The statistics of her disease, its pervasive growth, and rampant effect on her skin all pointed to a very serious form of the affliction, and suggested she was likely to be permanently disabled. Yet through the process of her healing, she defied all of those odds. When summer rolled around, and she went into the sun for the first time since her diagnosis, she stepped further outside of the bounds of expectation, and her doctors were dumbfounded by the extent of her recovery. Even the best-case scenario pointed to a lifelong scarring of her leg, but there is absolutely no evidence of her disease on that part of her body. Her primary rheumatologist even went so far as to question whether or not Sam had already begun to self-cure before we brought her in, which we knew wasn't true.

Then the start of this year began, and she was once again afflicted with a strange, obscure, and in this case, ultimately undiagnosed illness that ravaged her brain and body. The closest guess they had was a form of auto-encephalitis that has only been diagnosed a few thousand times in the United States since physicians gained the ability to detect it a few years ago. Even after months of treatment, complete healing from that illness isn't a certainly, and not everyone is able to return to their normal life afterward. In Samantha's case, since she was never diagnosed, she never received any form of treatment. She went to physical therapy for a few weeks to teach her how to walk again, but aside from that, there was nothing external to aid in her recovery.

Being afflicted with morphea in the first place was improbable, but the depth of her healing bordered on impossible. Her second disease is so rare that no one has even been able to identify what it is, but the treatment plan for the closest thing to her illness is extensive, invasive, and uncertain in terms of outcomes. The odds of both of those ailments hitting her and the odds of her recovering from both with nothing but intermittent dizziness and sensitivity to sounds lies deep in the realm of the statistically unimaginable.

When a song of Brandon's came on the radio earlier today and I remembered his story during the concert we'd attended, I heard the voice of God coming through loud and clear. He used math to demonstrate that He lies outside of what I can predict, quantify, or understand. In choosing that medium to display His power, He demonstrated that He knows me far better than anyone else. The words in the first half of Jeremiah 1:5 ring true, "Before I formed you in the womb I knew you, before you were born I set you apart." His miracles shine through in ways that allow me to see His elaborate knowledge of who I am and helps me to know that He is God.

# Chapter Thirty

# Actions Speak Louder

AT THE END of each business day, I make my way through the moderately crowded streets of downtown Houston, following a circuitous route to reach 59 North, which leads me back home for the evening. Along my path, there is a corner that is nearly always attended by a destitute man in his mid-forties. Houston has an enormous population of homeless people, so the sight of one in the downtown area isn't shocking or surprising; it's actually a bit alarming when I don't see a few on my drive to and from the office. This particular individual, however, has always been something of a standout; he has a bike. It's nothing fancy and in a terrible state of disrepair, but it's transportation of some sort, which has to be a coveted possession in the eyes of his peers. About once every two weeks, I notice that he has a flat tire, but the bike is still his, and I have no doubt he'll ride it on the rims when it comes time to head to his resting place each night.

We all have a natural disposition when it comes to the sight of the homeless, generally falling into one of two mind-sets. One group views those with cardboard signs as an opportunity to express kindness and compassion to people in an unfortunate situation. Others are quick to avoid eye contact and look upon those individuals with an air of disdain, viewing homelessness as more of a consequence of poor choices than uncontrollable circumstances. In all honesty, I usually fall into the latter of those two camps. I try to fight that tendency, at times carrying around gift cards for nearby fast-food restaurants but still remain highly reluctant to hand over cash, out of concern that I am contributing to some form of substance abuse or covertly rewarding someone for not being a productive member of society. There are even times, when my mood is overcast, that I scoff at those naive enough to hand over their hard-earned money, thinking to myself that they must be too ignorant to realize the foolishness of their actions. As I watch person after person, day after day, giving money to the man at the final turn before I head home, I sometimes glare with disapproval.

One recent evening, I made my usual trip through downtown and found myself at the same corner, the same homeless man in his usual spot; but on that day, something was different. As I stopped at the red light next to him, I saw the homeless man looking in the direction of his bike, his half-toothless mouth curled at the corners into a piratelike grin. His bike was broken down to the frame, both wheels removed, and a man dressed in black slacks and a long-sleeved blue shirt was kneeling beside it. He had disassembled the bike and was slowly replacing its two flat tires with new ones, likely putting it in the finest state it had seen for quite some time. His sleeves rolled up, his hands coated in grease, his brow matted with sweat-tinged hair, he wasn't handing over any cash, but he was giving richly.

In my upper middle-class suburb, we are quick to give financially but far less interested in getting our hands dirty. Schedules are already overloaded with business trips and long hours consuming most of our free time. Gymnastics, swim team practices, the endless circuit of birthday parties, and time spent at church takes what little remains. As a result, picking up a checkbook is far easier than rolling up our sleeves, so we take the wide path of donating more often than the narrow path of doing. This divergence of thought and action is one that seems increasingly prevalent in our society and is wildly different from the examples we have in both the Old and New Testament.

Most of the Jews of that period viewed thought and action as intimately entwined. What you felt, you did, and vice versa. For someone to claim a set of beliefs and not see those beliefs displayed in their daily lives bordered on heresy. In looking at the life of Christ, He may have told a lot of parables, but He was a man of action. His claim of divinity wasn't simply the result of Him quoting scripture; it was the product of turning Old Testament prophecy into an observable, tangible reality. He didn't simply avoid temptation; He subjected Himself to forty days of it to mature spiritually. He didn't parlay about the miraculous; He performed healings and resurrections. He didn't suggest the presence of demons; He called them by name and cast them into the darkness from which they came. He even openly chastised the religious elite who had begun to separate thought and action, accusing them of failing to live as God expected, and for that, they sought to destroy Him.

They despised Him for His words but feared Him for His ability to accomplish feats with divine power. Ultimately, He didn't express His thoughts on what crucifixion would be like and how it might offer salvation if only someone would take up that cross. He allowed Himself to be sacrificed to serve His purpose in carrying out the will of God and provide salvation for all who follow Him. It is action that defines who we are, action that allows the world to see past our thoughts and into our souls.

Yesterday, for the first time since her second illness, Samantha was willing to talk about the early days of her sickness. In late January and early February, things were at their worst; her mental capacity reduced to that of an infant and her memory seemingly wiped clean for hours or days on end. Sam has a deep and seemingly limitless love for her brother, so even during the darkest of days, she would call him "No-No" or "Brother" when Noah was beyond her ability to recall. As she sat on her brother's bed yesterday, we spoke for a few moments about the days that passed almost six months earlier.

"Sam, were there times when you didn't know Noah's name?" I asked.

"Yes," she replied, "I couldn't always remember what to call him. That's why sometimes I said 'No-No' or 'Brother.'"

"But even without knowing his name, you always knew who he was, right?"

Smiling, she said, "Of course, I love my brother too much to not know him."

Part of me knew the answer to the question I was to ask, but I pressed a bit further, "What about Mom and Dad, did you always remember who we were?"

She slowly pulled her knees to her chest, her chin nearly resting on them as she closed herself off, an answer in and of itself.

"It's OK, kiddo, you aren't in trouble, and no one will be upset with you if you didn't remember, but you're the only one who knows what happened in your mind, and I'm just trying to understand it better."

She began to shake her head side to side, "No, I didn't always remember."

I slid a hand along her arm, trying to reassure her, "I already knew that, you just hadn't said it quite yet. So when you couldn't remember who we were, how did you know we were your mom and dad?"

Her answer was elegant in its simplicity. "Because of what you did. You always took care of me and always loved me, so I knew you were different from everyone else."

I haven't yet shared that conversation with Beth; I don't know if I will before she reads it here. Part of it will break her heart, knowing our little girl couldn't remember who we were. Hopefully, the part that conveys her undying devotion to caring for her ailing daughter and that she was seen as a light in the darkness during that time will outweigh the sting of Sam's confession. I see her words as a testament to the power of stepping beyond esoteric thoughts and into tangible action. Anyone could have said "I love you" to her, but only her mother and father would have stayed by her side every waking moment in the hospital, through all the tests and doctor's visits, through the violent temper tantrums, and cared for her in the way we did.

As it is with many things, I don't think most people stop moving from thought to action out of ill intent. We rationalize that we're too busy, that we aren't as capable as others, or that our priorities simply don't allow for a divergence from our routines. As a result, we begin to think more but do less. In time, that practice becomes a habit, and soon, we find our hands entirely devoid of grease and free from calluses. We hear the phrase "Actions speak louder than words," and completely agree that everyone else should do a better job of writing checks the way that we do and cast a few stones from the comfort of our glass houses. A businessman's filthy hands and a homeless man's smile comingled with a little girl's faith in her unknown, nameless caregivers are quick to shatter that perspective. It's not what we say, not even what we give; it's what we do that shows the world the depth of our hearts. Our actions either convey or fail to convey the type of love Christ came to show us before His final, sacrificial demonstration. He provided the ultimate example of how far love will go to reach the least of us, homeless men and sick little girls included.

As with every other struggle I've highlighted in the chapters before this one, I don't expect to be cured of my pessimistic disposition in an instant. I will continue to fail, will continue to judge, will continue to scoff; but I also plan on putting a few rags in the trunk, just in case I'm bold enough to get my hands dirty one of these days.

# Chapter Thirty-One

# No End in Sight

I N OUR FLEETING, temporal perspective on the world that surrounds us, we instinctively seek closure. We crave finality to the various phases in our lives that serve as the end of a given chapter and allow us to start another. To this chapter, however, there may be no end.

Samantha has improved by leaps and bounds since her brain was ravaged by disease, but her healing is not complete, as it appears to be with her morphea. The sound of an air compressor, the pressure of a plane descending from its cruising altitude, even an errant (or perhaps intentional) punch to the head while wrestling with her brother all cause another regression. I watch with a pained heart as she attempts to tie her shoes, only to look at me with tear-filled eyes and ask for help when she realizes she doesn't remember how to do it on her own. A mere fifteen minutes later, the fog clears, and she is back to herself, but the frustration from her inability a few moments before still lingers.

The closest thing to which I can compare it is a snow globe. As it rests undisturbed on the shelf, nothing seems amiss; the statuette before me sits in perfect tranquility, every detail of it crystal clear. Then some external stimulus sends tremors through the placid waters, and the thing so easily visible a moment earlier becomes obscured by the flurry of dormant particles that were lying in wait all along. In time, the swirling stops, the particles settle, and all is clear again, but you know that another ripple can cause the interference to emerge anew. Any parent would want to steady that shelf; it seems unnatural not to painstakingly seek out anything that causes instability or disruption and avoid it at all costs.

I know all too well that releasing perceived control is an exceptionally difficult task. In a culture that praises the do-it-yourself mind-set, the hubris that develops can be very dangerous. We view problems as challenges that lie in vacuums, with the repercussions of constant probing, experimenting, and manipulating falling to the wayside as minor forms of collateral damage. In my case, however, honing in so heavily on Sam's illnesses that I fail to see my obsession's effect on my daughter's emotional and spiritual development is a disservice to her. Chastising Beth for turning on a blender without warning or berating my son for an accidental collision with Samantha's head does a disservice to both of them. Forgetting that God possesses an ability to heal her that extends well beyond my ability to understand is a disservice to my faith. I struggle with the fatherly need to fix her and the Christian's creed of letting my cares rest on the shoulders of one greater than I. It doesn't matter that I've known more peace in those brief periods of respite when I lay that burden down than I've known in combing through medical records and abstracts of studies; the innate compulsion to problem solve remains.

In her own way, my wife's sagacity comes in handy at times like these. The part of me that remains concerned about Sam's well-being watches for the slightest reactions, the triggers that cause them, how best to avoid them, or identify the part of her brain that's being affected. But every once in a while, Beth rests a hand on my shoulder and knowingly reminds me that my obsession puts a negative spotlight on Sam each time I do that, a behavior that is potentially more damaging to her self-esteem and recovery than the period of regression she experiences.

With the exception of times when my insomnia runs rampant and the occasional flustering that only my wife can summon, I am slow to react and even slower to anger—externally, at least. But when injustice occurs and the individual on the receiving end of that equation is a child, I have no patience whatsoever. My reaction is immediate, harsh, and consistent; the kind of person who would willingly cause a child to suffer needn't be a part of this world once his or her crimes are realized. That makes for a rather quizzical circumstance when the suffering a child experiences is caused by a disease that lies within her. It is particularly troublesome for those who attribute all things, whether we perceive them as good or bad, to be intentional actions carried out by God. I can read all of the verses I want speaking of wisdom, can admit my own lack of understanding about God's ultimate will, and can even find the silver lining in many circumstances. Yet at the deepest levels of my soul, I cannot find peace when a child suffers. My attitude is akin to Ivan's in *The Brothers Karamazov,* by Fyodor Dostoyevsky, when he argues with his brother, Alyosha, on the subject of children who suffer and the role that plays in the harmony that awaits us in the world beyond this one.

> "But then there are the children, and what am I to do about them? That's a question I can't answer. For the hundredth time I repeat, there are numbers of questions, but I've only taken the children, because in their case what I mean is so unanswerably clear. Listen! If all must suffer to pay the price for the eternal harmony, what have children to do with it, tell me, please? It's beyond all comprehension why they should suffer, and why they should pay for the harmony . . . if the sufferings of children go to swell the sum of sufferings which was necessary to pay for truth, then I protest that the truth is not worth such a price." Alyosha responds a moment later with two words, "That's rebellion."

The mainstream world of Christianity would certainly side with the less verbose of the two brothers on this topic. Suggesting that the pains endured by a single child render any concept of ultimate peace null and void is met with chastising voices reminding us that there's much we don't have the purview to understand, that sufferings are temporal speed bumps on the highway to heaven, and that "this too shall pass." There are a myriad of verses in the New Testament related to that subject, telling us that suffering is spiritually beneficial, but in 1 Peter 4:13, we are told that it also affords us an opportunity to better identify with the pains Christ knew during his life on earth. As an adult, I can make some sense of that and don't shy away from the memory of pains that have befallen me over the years. But as a father, I can't even begin to grasp how to explain that to my little girl, who keeps asking me when she isn't going to be sick anymore. I try to find opportunities to explain to her that the trials of today provide chances for us to make choices that will bring joy to the lives of those around us and the God watching over us. Yet some part of me always remains at arm's length during those conversations, rejecting the idea that God should simply sit back and watch instead of stepping in and healing her. After reading a slew of stories from the New Testament, Samantha even said that she wished Jesus was on earth now so that she could go see him and be healed. But just as quickly as the words escaped her lips, she exhaled noisily, shrugged her shoulders, and said, "Just in case He doesn't, I'll keep hoping and praying that I feel better when I wake up tomorrow."

She goes to bed saying that at least two or three nights a week: "I hope and pray that I feel better when I wake up tomorrow." I long for that tomorrow with more fervor than I could possibly express, but it is yet to come. So while we wait for that day to arrive, I will try to set aside my rebellion and enjoy each moment to the fullest, focusing on where we are today, not eternally fixing my gaze on the potentially unreachable place we wish we could be.

I know that Christ spoke truth in Matthew 11:28–30 when He told His disciples to bring Him their burdens and trust them to the care of the Lord. It is with a reluctant but hopeful heart that I strive more each day to set aside my obsession with controlling her illnesses and instead focus my efforts on loving her as she is and ensuring I remain mindful of my role as the spiritual head of my house. Our family has endured much over the last three years, and I have no assurance that the hardest times are behind us. Yet the miracles around me are countless, if only I will open my eyes to see the healing each person in my family has experienced during this trying time.

I know that I will continue to fail, falter, and largely remain a shadow of the man God wishes me to be during life's trials and tribulations. I completely believe that it is only through humility and self-sacrifice that I can grow closer to becoming who I am designed to be.

No matter how hard it is, I will try to set aside my need for control. I will try to silence the rebellion within me when it rages with fury. I will try with every fiber of my being to hear God's whisper as it comes time and time again. If I ever hope to know true peace and joy, even in the darkest of nights, I will pray without ceasing, in the hopes that He will give me the strength to take His outstretched hand and abide in Him.

Made in the USA
Middletown, DE
06 November 2014